EXPERIENCE AND TRADITION

D1563136

STEPHEN BRECK REID

EXPERIENCE AND TRADITION

ABINGDON PRESS

Nashville

EXPERIENCE AND TRADITION

Copyright © 1990 by Abingdon Press

This book is printed on acid-free paper.

Library of Congress Cataloging-in-Publication Data

Reid, Stephen Breck.
    Experience and tradition : a primer in Black biblical hermeneutics
by Stephen Breck Reid.
        p.   cm.
    Includes bibliographical references.
    ISBN 0-687-12400-X (alk. paper)
    1. Bible—Hermeneutics.   2. Black theology.   I. Title.
BS476.R43   1990
220.6 ' 08996073—dc20   90-43485
                                                                                       CIP

MANUFACTURED IN THE UNITED STATES OF AMERICA

Dedicated to

John A. Hollar

and

John Gammie

In Memoriam

Acknowledgments

This is to express my grateful appreciation to several persons without whose aid and encouragement this book would never have been written and published:

To my black colleagues and other African American biblical scholars at Collegeville, Minnesota, and elsewhere whose conversations remain a refreshing stream of insight and encouragement.

To my colleagues at Pacific School of Religion and the Graduate Theological Union.

To Barbara Brown Zikmund and Neely McCarter.

To Davis Perkins, whose early support helped get this project started.

To Priscilla Stuckey Kaufman and Archie Smith, Jr. for reading drafts and providing helpful suggestions.

To William B. McClain, Wesley Theological Seminary, who read the manuscript and rendered invaluable editorial assistance.

To the Rev. J. Alfred Smith, Sr., pastor at Allen Temple Baptist Church, and the good people of that congregation who gave valuable feedback as I presented some of this material in a series of lectures.

Special thanks to my family: Kathy Reid, and Derek, Jacob, Carly and Jesse for their patience. When Daddy said, "I have to work on the book," usually, they understood.

Stephen Breck Reid

Contents

Chapter I

Introduction

Scripture, Experience, and Tradition:
A Quest for Identity

It's no secret that the Bible occupies a central place in the religious life of black Americans: depicted in the Bible are the experiences of many black people, from slavery onward: Egyptian bondage and oppression of the Israelites, deportation into Babylonian captivity, the request of their captors to sing "their songs" in a strange land, a mocked and crucified Jesus, and the bedevilment by principalities and powers of the present age. It was from the Bible that many black slaves learned to read and it was to the Bible that so many of them went to find guidance, comfort, a word of hope, and the promise of their deliverance from sin and slavery. The Bible has been the *source* of inspiration for poetry and song, as well as the inspiration for drama and sermon.

Cain H. Felder is right in his book, *Troubling Biblical Waters: Race, Class and Family*: "Blacks have developed an *experiential sympathy* with much of the Bible, which, in turn, receives their reverent attention as quite literally the revealed word of God."[1]

Black people have interpreted the Bible from their own

experience, and have sought the black church as a part of their identity formation. The black church has claimed their loyalty because it continues to be that community of faith where they could define and shape themselves in spite of what the dominant culture said about them. They were clear who they were because the church constantly reminded them who they were.

Professor Vincent Wimbush reminds us of the importance of the stories of the biblical word:

> Since most of the earliest African-American Christians had been denied, from the beginning of their experience in the Americas, the opportunity to be fully human, including the opportunity to learn to read and write, the "letters" of biblical texts were not crucial in their appropriation and redaction of Christian traditions. What became important was the *telling* and *retelling*, the hearing and re-hearing of biblical stories—stories of perseverance, of strength in weakness and under oppressive burdens, of hope in hopeless situations.[2]

But there are many modern demons present in our current age and American culture that threaten to possess us, and present a challenge to the black pastor and theologian. Like the Gerasene demoniac who answered Jesus' question, "What is your name?" by saying: "My name is Legion; for we are many" (Mark 5:1-20), the demons that threaten to possess us and destroy our tradition are multifaceted and legion. They threaten our identity and the black church tradition of interpretation and application of the scripture.

Perspective

The perspective of the black church springs from the life experience of black people. Black biblical interpretation begins with black experience. Black experience is not monolithic. Nonetheless, there remains a consistent perspective as we survey black church tradition.

Black experience may be interpreted in a number of ways, but there remains a common denominator: *The question of identity organizes black biblical interpretation.* As we focus on black identity, no attempt will be made to accentuate the differences between white Protestantism and black church tradition. We will break the identity question into two related parts: where our identity as a people begins and how we keep faith with our tradition.

The question of identity resounds in our ears as we hear the sound of the ocean and picture ourselves on the slave ships. The black church began as a slave church. Black biblical *hermeneutics* must reach back to the antiquity of our oppression. The black biblical scholar is a detective who must discover anew the tradition of scripture in the black church and culture. Any black biblical hermeneutic must be tested by the blood of antiquity. The blood of black Christians in North Africa and Ethiopia and the blood of black Christians shed in the red clay of Georgia and Alabama are the litmus tests of any black biblical theology.

The challenge of our identity as a slave church mandates the affirmation of unity; God cannot be fragmented. There is no discontinuity; time cannot be torn apart, but is rather like a flowing stream. Therefore, the ancient blood of black Christians witnesses for or against any black biblical theology in the present.

During my graduate school experience, I attended a class in which the professor and a white student once discussed what was wrong with contemporary American culture. The theme of this conversation was that too many people were talking about their rights and not enough about their responsibilities. They implied that those "too many people" were young or black or women.

At that moment, I heard the blood of black folks cry out from the earth, "Don't you believe this!" Just as the blood of the innocent Abel cried from the ground (Gen. 4:10), so also the blood of black people cried for justice. The black preachers and biblical scholars have only to listen to the voices of the black saints. The affirmation of unity with the past in black biblical hermeneutics confronts the destructive power and politics of much of contemporary biblical criticism.

Like the Gerasene demoniac, and like other black people in the United States, I live with the threat of possession. The demon has many manifestations. The black church reads the Bible in order to stave off the challenge of popular political theology.

One reader of an early draft of this book argued that I was confusing popular Christianity with American civil religion, the latter being a political theology. She maintained that from the perspective of the working theologian such a combination is incorrect. She could not have been more wrong.

A black perspective notices that popular Christianity has resulting politics. We need not call it civil religion, but popular Christianity remains a political theology. In fact, popular Christianity breeds a *popular political theology* because it understands certain power relationships as being appropriate and others as being inappropriate. Appropriate for the dominant group to have power; inappropriate for the poor and minorities to share in that power.

Such a position becomes demonic as black people internalize the popular political theology. The political interest of such popular theology attempts to squelch the sound of God's gospel of freedom for black people through a theology that says, "Everything is all right. Things are the way they should be." When we internalize this theology, we commit theological suicide.

Several years ago, Joseph Washington, in his book *Black Religion*, raised the issue of the danger of "black folk religion." He maintained that the challenge to the black church was to provide a good theology rather than an uncritical religion. This book echoes the challenge in new ways. We dare not internalize the popular political theology. It is heresy. It is death.

Black biblical interpretation undergirds the commitment to fight the internalization of popular political theology. Martin Luther King, Jr., stands in a long line of preachers who remind us of this challenge. The mechanism for freedom includes the affirmation of unity of black religious and political tradition.

Black oratory and worship in the black church provide a repository of black biblical reflection. The repository continues to illustrate the persistence of the black church to deny the popular political theology and to let scripture provide the intellectual bulwark for such a denial.

Biblical and theological interpretation are not located only in the past. It gives a perspective which enables the black interpreter to examine texts which are not necessarily familiar in the black church tradition. Unity affirms the natural contacts of religion and politics.

Black biblical hermeneutics, like those of any oppressed people, is ultimately the quest for identity as God's believing community. This entails the interpretation of black experience, which calls for the interpretation of other data, as well as scripture.[3] A black biblical hermeneutic must interpret both black experience and the biblical text.

The quest for our identity as the believing people of God focuses the attention of the black church. Our focus and commitment as God's people dictate the priorities for black biblical scholars and theologians. We can discern a common perspective, and from this perspective we can outline the common characteristics of the black experience.

The common characteristics of black church experience signal what God has planned for us as a believing black community. This volume focuses on black church identity. It maintains that scripture provides the vehicle for the investigation of identity, and that Black church tradition informs the interpretation of scripture.

Identity and interpretation always inform one another. The task of a black biblical hermeneutic involves the interpretation of black culture and the biblical text. Neither identity nor interpretation takes priority; they acts as partners. The black biblical scholar, theologian, and preacher holds black culture and tradition in the one hand and the Bible in the other.

Characteristics and Themes

Black experience has three characteristics, each of which has a thematic biblical element as well as cultural residue. The first characteristic of black experience affirms the unity of life. God's activity in the lives of black people spans culture, religion, and politics. The second characteristic of black experience recognizes that the black American community remains remarkably patriotic in the face of racism. The third characteristic is a sense of critical awareness of the promises of the Declaration of Independence and the Constitution yet to be fully realized for persons of color. This third characteristic blends critical awareness with racial pride and identity. Each characteristic can also be understood as a theme. UNITY Life presents us with a patchwork quilt. The political and the spiritual form the pieces of the quilt. To have one piece without the other leaves one not with a quilt, but with a collection of rags. The black church creates a quilt out of different and sometimes contradictory pieces of black experience. Hence, the affirmation of the unity of life comes to the fore.

PATRIOTISM AND LOYALTY The second characteristic of black experience recognizes the paradox of black patriotism. Earlier in this century, W. E. Burghardt DuBois, a noted black sociologist, proposed that patriotism and black liberation go hand in hand, just as the prophet Jeremiah (Jer. 29) instructed the exiles of Judah to work for the benefit of the Babylonian community.[4]

CRITICAL AWARENESS AND RACE PRIDE The third characteristic of black experience brings a critical awareness and an activism, called race pride. Black biblical interpretation sees the truth of justice as paramount. Such insight judges the falsehood of oppressive structures and their supporting theology. Like Job, the black community notices that suffering does not begin with the political action of the victim. The works righteousness model of religion and politics blames black people for the economic and social results of racism. But, critical awareness and race pride affirm the goodness of God's creation, including a people who are black. Critical awareness and race pride lead to the death of false piety of the conventional white religion. We do not say that God made a mistake in making people of many colors. In fact, such a beautiful and diverse creation is all the more reason to sing God's praises.

Chapter II

Reading the Bible in the Black Church

A Quest for Method

To properly investigate the themes of black experience, we must first have an appropriate method. Black church tradition reflects a struggle concerning the proper mechanism for delineating, understanding, and appropriating the three characteristics of black experience. The struggle shapes the quest for method. No one method can encompass the complexity of black experience. Many techniques are used in the patterning of a single quilt. Black church experience and the God of freedom we serve stand beyond the confines of any techniques we use. However, the reality of black church experience and the God of freedom affect every interpretative method used by black biblical scholars and theologians. A black church perspective interacts dynamically with the three characteristics of black experience.

Interpreting scripture provides a helpful model for interpreting the black experience for all of the themes are present. But a method of interpreting scripture, a black biblical hermeneutic, must interpret the black experience and the text as well. It is a two-fold task: To engage in serious dialogue with the text while showing how the biblical witness becomes adaptable for the fulfillment of human potential and the development of a community of life and faith in a racially hostile social, economic and political environment.

Methods and Movements

The application of black scriptural interpretation involves a consistent perspective and a flexible method. Whether one uses form criticism, canonical criticism or some other critical apparatus, these must conform to the method most fitting for the black church. Three movements constitute the method of black hermeneutics: a critical reading of the text; the recovery of black interpretation of the text; and the application of the text to the life experience of the black community.

These three movements are more like an equilateral triangle than a line of sequential steps. The biblical interpreter can enter at any one of the three points in the triangle. A critical reading of the text need not be prior to the recovery of black biblical interpretation of the material. Sometimes in the life of the church one will begin with an examination of how the application of the biblical message in everyday life corresponds to the interpretation.

The first movement consists of the *critical reading of the text.* In this movement we explore the material setting of the text, that is, the physical and social surroundings that influenced the writers of the text.[1] The critical reading investigates the way in which the material culture and social stratification interacted to form the community of faith that shaped the text. Critical reading enables the black church to be more aware of power relationships which are inappropriate for the community of faith.[2]

The term *critical* frightens some people. They think it means an attack on the scriptures. But a critical reading of the text functions as an assessment of our lives and the structures of sin. Hans Reudi Weber introduces his book, *Experiments in Bible Study*, with a story of a woman in an African village who was known for always reading her Bible. One day some of the village people asked why she read only the Bible. Her response was quick and to the point: "There are many books that I could read, but there is only one Book that reads me."[3] She described the critical reading of the Bible.

A critical reading of the Bible becomes an act of *conscientization*. This term, often used by Paulo Freire, best known for his work, *Pedagogy of the Oppressed*, is an expression of unmasking lies that are the cornerstone of the ideology of oppression.[4]

The second movement involves *the recovery of black interpretation of the text*. The critical reading of the text attends to the way it construes power relationships. The recovery of the black interpretation of the text examines the ways the black church and the black culture have interpreted biblical themes in order to reshape the power relationships of the believing community. Whenever we read a text, we have two readings: the intrinsic reading, seeing the passage only from its perspective; and the extrinsic perspective, reading the passage in the light of other related stories.

We have several examples of black interpretation of scripture other than commentary or sermon. For instance, the Joseph story reshapes the traditional laws and customs of inheritance. Joseph, who as the youngest brother was not in line for the inheritance, and was even sold by his jealous brothers into slavery in Egypt, becomes the bearer of salvation history (Gen. 37; 39-41).

Similarly, the Judah-Tamar story (Gen. 38) encourages one to reconsider the place of women.

This second movement amplifies the concerns of the themes of black interpretation of scripture. The affirmation of unity as a central theme of black experience accents the importance of culture, for culture provides artistic and literary expression to the unity of life. Black interpretation of scripture does not end with the spirituals and sermons of the black church. Black literary tradition, from its inception to the present, has struggled with interpretation of biblical themes. We shall focus particularly on the struggle with the biblical themes in black literature.

The recovery of black interpretation of biblical themes involves not only commentaries and books as resources, where these are available, but also the poetry and music of the black church and community. Poetry and music have long been forms of black biblical interpretation; the spiritual "Dry Bones" interprets Ezek. 37.[5]

The recovery of biblical tradition does not mean that the material is self-consciously interpreting a given biblical text. Sometimes the material reflects on biblical themes in the black community.

The second movement in recovering black biblical tradition creates solidarity through the use of memory. The recollection of tradition binds the black community. "Anamnesis [memory] is not merely a recollection of past sufferings, it is also a rediscovery of the meaning of the church's task in the present time. Anamnestic solidarity can be a basis for hope in the present."[6] By focusing on the black interpretation of scripture, we see how the memory of the Hebrews informed blacks from slavery to the present and forged a solidarity between the Hebrews' salvation history and that of blacks. Thus a new solidarity through memory becomes possible.

Each chapter of this book will demonstrate a different

way to work with the recovery of black biblical tradition. Chapter 3 will illustrate how this might be done with poetry and novels. Chapter 4 will explore the use of black music in the interpretation of biblical themes. Chapter 5 will investigate black drama and biblical themes.[7]

The third movement involves the *application of the text to the life experience of the black community*. The Bible remains a practical instrument for faith and practice in black church tradition. Most discussions of the agenda of black churches ultimately revert to a discussion of the biblical foundations for such an action, and the strategy for the material reform and revolution in black communities emerges. Black biblical hermeneutics and theology must constantly seek to find roots in a practical and pastoral theology. Biblical theology and hermeneutics, in a practical sense, begins when one attempts to implement biblical faith.

Our focus here, nonetheless, addresses practical theology less than biblical reflection. Therefore, the application sections at the end of each chapter are more illustrative than exhaustive.

Three subsequent chapters will illuminate the way that the perspective and method of reading the Bible in the black church counters the internalization of popular political theology. The first chapter explores pastoral theology. The second investigates homiletical and liturgical theology, and the third examines political and economic theology.

Christological Issues

The Christ event binds the black church together. Therefore, the interpreter and the method must address the christological question, no matter what the biblical text may be. Much of black biblical tradition springs from the Hebrew Bible (most often referred to as the Old Testament). Nevertheless, each text and theme will be tested by the Christ event.

One evening at a dinner party, some seminarians were talking about sermons. One woman asked me whether my sermons had a "JPL." For a while I kept quiet, until it became clear that I was going to have to ask what a "JPL" was. It seems that the African Methodist Episcopal woman who taught preaching had told her students, "In the black church, if you do not have a Jesus Punch Line, you have not preached." Just as a punch line is the pay off for a joke, so also the christological reflection brings together the theological importance of the biblical reading.

Each chapter of this book contains a reflection on the christological issues. The issue of christology in the black church has many dimensions. We will focus on only two recurring questions. The first question comes from the tradition of the imitation of Christ, *imitatio christi*, in the life of the church. How are we to conform our lives to the will of God, demonstrated by the example of Christ? The second question comes from the tradition of the victorious Christ, *christus victor*. What are the political effects of the reign of God?

We have discovered that the problem of the black church is the temptation to internalize popular political theology. This problem orients the black church perspective. Out of that perspective three characteristics and themes emerge: (1.) unity, (2.) patriotism and loyalty, and (3.) critical awareness and racial pride.

The black church perspective also generates a method to examine these characteristics and themes. The method includes three movements: critical reading of the text (*intrinsic reading*), recovery of the black biblical interpretation of the text (*extrinsic reading*), and the application of the reading to action.

Since black church tradition demands that we have a Jesus Punch Line, we will examine black biblical hermeneutics through the exploration of three themes and three movements and will conclude with a christological reflection.

Every movement provides the interpreter with an opportunity to listen to the voices of black tradition and culture. Every movement challenges the interpreters to articulate a voice for material reform and revolution. Here the music, literature, and art of black tradition stand as invaluable conversation partners. Also, the black strategy for change of B. T. Washington, W. E. B. DuBois, Marcus Garvey, Martin Luther King, Jr., Jesse Jackson, and others must be heard as we apply the Scripture to everyday life in a society bedeviled by oppression, racism, and an insidious popular theology that threatens to silence the gospel of freedom and liberation in favor of the noise of "sounding brass" and the "tinkling cymbal" of the dominant culture.

Post Script

Almost every black writer struggles with the issue of white readers. The question of what makes such a stance more than an intellectual curiosity for the non-black community must be addressed. As noted above, the primary focus of this book concerns how the Bible informs black church experience. Nonetheless, a black biblical hermeneutic must uncover the truth. Black interpretation of scripture must preach the gospel—not just the truth for the black community and not just the gospel for the black church. When we embrace the truth of the gospel, and apply it to our lives and our society, "all flesh shall see it together." For the truth, which is Truth, shall make all free.

Chapter III

Unity

The Foundation of a Black Hermeneutic

Unity of life provides the foundation for black interpretation of scripture. The interpretative themes of loyalty and critical awareness rest on this foundation. Black experience requires that we define unity as the interplay of cultural and material life. The cultural life is found in the music, art, literature, and theology of black culture. This maintains black identity as independent of white culture. Cultural life forms the intellectual furniture for black life.

Material life is the socio-economic realities of black life. Here the realities of the interplay of racism and capitalism in America make themselves known. Racial discrimination is an economic fact. Material *life* provides a "feeling" environment of black life.

Unity, that is the interplay of culture and material life, finds expression in scripture as well as black life. This scriptural affirmation becomes an indication of more faithful interpretation of scripture in the black church. The message of the Rev. Dr. Martin Luther King, Jr. rings with the theme of unity. Peace, justice, and jobs, the code words for the theme of unity in the black experience provides an ever-present witness and a resounding chorus in black church tradition.

Unity plays an important role in black church tradition. The interdependence of black *pietism* and black radicalism points to this unity. Black Christian radicalism always stand in the midst of black christology of *imitatio christi* and *christus victor*. Black radicalism affirms that we imitate Jesus in our movement toward justice. Further, that movement has credibility due to the efficacy of the resurrection and the victorious Christ.

Unity Based on the Doctrine of God

Unity in the black church springs from an understanding of God and our response to the integrity of God. God's integrity requires our affirmation of the unity of life. An examination of Deut. 6:4-5 makes this point with incisive clarity.

> Hear, Israel, the Lord is our God, the Lord is one.
> Therefore, you shall love the Lord with *all* your heart,
>   *all* your mind, and *all* your strength.

The passage continues with admonition for Israel to put the words of God upon their hearts. The Hebrew term for heart, *leb,* is the seat of the will, not vague feelings. Inscribed on the black marble will of black people are the words of God.

The writer, to accent this, assures that these words are with us in our working, resting, getting up, and lying down. This means that God's words become a perspective. This is all the more clear when we notice that the commandments are between the eyes.

Hermeneutics is not a new method, or thought, it is a perspective. And black biblical hermeneutics is a new vision, a new way of seeing which changes all methods.

Unity Based in Creation Theology

Black communities experience unity in three distinct, but interconnected, movements. The first movement is the awareness of unity as a possibility through partnership between God and humans, between humans and the earth, and between women and men. The second movement witnesses the blocks to unity and partnership. A third movement envisions the recovery of unity and partnership.

PARTNERSHIP James Weldon Johnson articulated the unity of black experience in his work *God's Trombones*. An analysis of his work will demonstrate that unity has expression in black church tradition as partnership. The nexus of relation and action constitute partnership. The action dimension moves from motivation to deliberation and action. The poem, "The Creation," opens with God's motivation: Creation begins with God's search for community as he steps out on space, looks around, and says,

> I'm lonely—
> I'll make me a world.

Unity, according to black church tradition, affirms the oneness of human life. As in the examination of the doctrine of God, we see that the unity of human life springs from a creation theology as well. Creation begins and remains the search for integrity and relationship. When action and relationship are joined, we have a partnership.

A. Partnership Rooted in Divine Activity

Johnson, in his interpretation of Gen. 1, portrays unity as an expression of partnership. Divine activity provides the catalyst for partnership. White tradition focuses on

27

God's creation through *word*. Johnson, on the other hand, accents the *activity* of God in creation.

Johnson accents God's action beyond the creation through speech. He describes God's first action: God smiles. God creates, not by word, but by smile. Johnson uses the line "And God said: That's Good!" as a parentheses to the description of the early divine action. In between the parentheses, Johnson inserts action verbs: reach out, took, rolled, and hurled. God creates through word and other action verbs in black church tradition.

B. Partnership through Relationships

But the story does not end with the creation and redemption of the earth. God creates the human community, thus setting up a nexus of key relationships.

Here we see the divine activity energizing the relationships. God creates the human out of the soil that God had redeemed through the rain. God's hands shape the creation of the human community. The hands of God get dirty in the process of creating humans.

1. Motivation.

The reason for this quality of divine activity is clear in black church tradition. Even God yearns for relationship. Hence, Johnson returns to the theme of loneliness as a motivation for God's action. The pivotal words are, "I'm lonely still."

2. Deliberation.

The scripture describes the act of creation of humans as a natural next step. Johnson, on the other hand, accents the brooding and ponderously deliberative process that leads to the creation of the human community.

3. Action.

Johnson stresses the intimacy of God's action in the creation of the human community. God sat down on a hill before thinking of the creation of humanity.

Johnson affirms the human community by accenting the greatness of God and God's activity. He further affirms the human community through his deliberate focus on the labor of God on the human's behalf; bending, kneeling, toiling, and shaping. If the great and Almighty God created us as black folks with such assiduous attention and toil, then we must be valuable. If God has labored over us with such intricate detail, molding and making us, then we must be dear to the heart of God.

Johnson's interpretation of the creation story draws on unity in the partnership metaphor. Action and relation combine in this partnership. He divides the action into motivation and deliberation, thus depicting God's search for relationship and community resulting in the creation of the human community.

The critical reading of any biblical text must begin with an examination of the socio-political context of the passage. The material in Gen. 2-4 was brought together by the Yahwist, a tenth-century collection of editors sponsored by kings David and Solomon. The goal of this material was to validate the social order of tenth century B.C.E. Israel. In order to accomplish this task, the stories describe tenth-century practices and label them as the will of God from the beginning.

Genesis 2 provides an exception to the general tone of the material, describing a lost sexual equality. It provides an alternative to the male hierarchical structure of the Israelite state. This chapter pictures partnership in three ways: the subservient role of persons as creatures made by God; the relationship between the human community and the environment; and a community of women and

29

men living in equality. Humans are made by God, from the earth, and for one another as partners.

Humans are made by God. No human directs the action in Gen. 2; God directs the action. God forms *ha'adam.* God breathes life into *ha'adam* so that it might become a "living being." God makes the woman. The black church affirms people as creatures of God who are valued as the recipients of God's act of redemption through creation.

The Hebrew text of Gen. 2 accents God's activity in the process of the creation of the human community. Just as God had "caused it to rain" so also God now "formed" the human. The verb for "informed" (*yasar*) means to mold as a potter does with clay. This points to divine activity. Any black preacher would remind us that we cannot throw [mold] a pot from clay without getting our hands dirty with the clay. Likewise, the hands of God are touched by the messy act of creation.

Humans are made from the earth. God forms *ha'adam* from *ha'adamah*, the soil. Thus, the text sharply focuses the relationship between the human community and the environment. The land will witness the atrocities of humans (Gen. 4) and provide food for the humans (Gen. 3). The humans are made from and connected to the earth.

Humans are made for each other in community. Humanity, like God, moves in a world of relationships. God created humans because of a need for relationship. The loneliness of God is mirrored in the loneliness of *ha'adam.* The phrase "it is not good for *ha'adam* [sometime translated 'the man'] to be alone" points to the need for partnership. The creature needs an *'ezer kenegdo.* The RSV translates this as "helper fit for."

The term *'ezer,* helper, means more than a servant. Scripture describes God as a helper (See Exod. 18:4; Deut. 33:29). One can not make a case that a helper is a person with less power than another. The notion of "helper" being subordinate propels both sexism and racism. The connection between racism and sexism makes this a crucial point in the life of the black church. Women and people of color are continually described as helpers and servants. Where one finds 'ezer translated as "helper" in the sense of a servant, one will find fertile ground for growing racism as well as sexism. The "helper" in this model does not shape history, the "helper" can only assist those who do shape history. Once this is ordained by God, it becomes incumbent on the powerful men of the society to label women and people of color as something less. "Helper" belies a power relationship.

The preposition kenegdo, "over against," speaks eloquently of the power relationship. The preposition pictures an encounter in which equals and full partners stand face-to-face.

God knits together the bond of partnership of women and men. Ha'adam [the man] did not create the woman, and the writer accents this. Ha'adam [the man] is asleep (Gen. 2:21) when this act of creation takes place. Black men do not create black women; God creates each for partnership.

The partnership continues in the description of the creation. The woman is created through the first surgery. The reader imagines God's opening the man's flesh, reaching in and taking the necessary portion. The reader remembers that there is a lot of messy stuff below the surface of the skin. The very hands of God participate in this messy process: the clay and the surgery. God creates through a messy process both men and women. Thereby, God participates intensively in both acts of creation and emphasizes the equal partnership.

When seeing the woman of his life who is to be his partner, Adam breaks into spontaneous poetry which

31

accents their relationship: "This at last is bone of my bones and flesh of my flesh" (Gen. 2:23a).

The sexual equality causes some shifts in power (Gen. 2:24-25) and black men and women stand naked and unashamed. Few metaphors elicit as strong a response for the daughters and sons of slaves than nudity. Frequently in the slave experience, nudity was forced. Nakedness constituted a visible symbol of the vulnerability and powerlessness of the slave. Neither black men nor black women could prevent the public display of their sexuality for public inspection.

The vulnerability that accompanies nudity did not escape the writers of the Bible. The Hebrew words for nudity ('erom, 'arom, 'ervah) occur approximately seventy times in the Hebrew Bible, almost a third of those appearing in the book of Leviticus. The other occurrences consistently use nudity as a symbol of vulnerability In the book of Job the references demonstrate Job's nakedness at birth and at death, the most vulnerable of times (Job 1:21; 22:6; 24:7, 10; 26:6). They mark the entrance and exit of this life and community. Also the Bible notes that even the land can be vulnerable and naked (Gen. 42:9, 12).

The vulnerability of nudity often connotes shame. In Isa. 20:2, 4, the Assyrians paraded their captives back to Assyrian naked as a form of humiliation. Vulnerability without partnership generates shame. Whether it be Assyrian or Babylonian exiles or black slaves, this imposed vulnerability became a source of shame used as a vehicle for social control.

The writer of the Gen. 2 passage maintains that there can be such a thing as appropriate vulnerability, and nudity expresses this. Appropriate vulnerability does not carry with it shame. Partnership represents the key that opens to black women and men a world of appropriate vulnerability.

Summary. Three key partnerships exist in Gen. 2: God

makes a partnership with women and men through the act of creation. The act of creation forms a partnership between the human community and the environment. Adam and Eve, representing men and women, from the beginning are partners of each other. The idea of partnership in black church tradition could not escape the image of Jesus. If God is the head of the firm, then Jesus is surely the senior partner.

BLOCKS TO PARTNERSHIP: THE BREAKDOWN OF THE CREATED ORDER There are blocks that unify the black experience to partnership. In a racist society, structured poverty, racism and sexism constitute the pillars that block unity in partnership. These blocks come in two categories: interpersonal blocks, as well as structural and corporate blocks.

The Rhinoceros: Interpersonal Blocks to Partnership

One day a sex therapist came into a sexual ethics class. She described herself as a rhinoceros tamer, explaining that most couples who experience sexual dysfunction have a rhinoceros in bed with them. The rhinoceros represents something external to the couple that blocks their relationship. For most black Americans, the problems created by racism are our rhinoceroses.

The rhinoceros is one way to describe the "other" that has a great impact on relationship. The "other" need not even be present to shape the relationship. It is an ever-present compulsion to be someone else and to want something external to ourselves to give us value. The rhinoceros brings us a sense of self-hate that penetrates to the core of our sexuality. We hate not only ourselves but also those who remind us of ourselves. Adam hated Eve. Cain hated Abel. The "other", *daimon*, rhinoceros makes all this possible.

The novelist Toni Morrison, in *The Bluest Eye,* tells the story of Pecola, an eleven-year-old black girl who desperately wants to have blue eyes. Pecola's friend, Claudia, serves as narrator of most of the story. The problem began with a blue-eyed baby doll. Eventually, Claudia begins to attack all non-white beauty by destroying white baby dolls (pp. 19-20).

The fascination concerning the power of white beauty persists. Reflecting that power is Maureen Peal a white girl who enchants the children at school. And Maureen does just that; she peels away the layers of protective armor to uncover the self-hate of the black children. For example, she notices that the name Pecola was used for the daughter in the movie, "Imitation of Life," the daughter who passed for white (p. 57). "And all the time we knew that Maureen Peal was not the Enemy and not worthy of such intense hatred. The *Thing* to fear was the *Thing* that made *her* beautiful and us not" (p. 62). Pecola wants blue eyes. She wants to be somebody else. When the black people who populate her world talk about wanting to "be somebody," they mean they want to be "somebody else."

Pecola could come to grips with marginality, or she could go mad in the face of absurdity. Thus are the choices put before us by the rhinoceros of racism. Pecola demonstrates in graphic terms what marginality is a life on the edge or outside. Her family, the Breedloves, lived in a storefront under a brothel. Morrison uses the "ugliness" of Pecola's life to demonstrate how she was socially marginalized, outside.

The dominant culture had pronounced them ugly, and they found no evidence to contradict that, not even religion. Their ugliness was a given from God, according to the religion of the "Master."
Pecola hid herself. For according the rhinoceros, the "other," she belonged outside. Finding herself always on the outside, Pecola comes to live with Claudia and her family because Pecola's drunken father has put the

Breedloves "outdoors," has caused their eviction. "Outdoors, we knew, was the real terror of life" (p. 17).

The marginality of the "outdoors" remains a fact of black existence. "Dead doesn't change and outdoors is here to stay." This engenders the drive to have things. "Knowing that there was such a thing as outdoors bred in us a hunger for property, for ownership" (p. 18).

The story of Pecola's first menstruation is a foreshadowing of her fertility, actualized in her subsequent pregnancy. The first menstruation strikes awe into the girls. Claudia explains to Pecola that menstruation indicates the ability to bear children. Pecola naturally begins to question where children come from. Claudia frames the answer in terms of "love." "Then Pecola asked a question that had never entered my mind. 'How do you do that, I mean, how do you get someone to love you?' But Freida was asleep and I didn't know" (p. 29) "Love" here acts as a euphemism for sexual intercourse. However, the novel continually asks the question "how do you get some one to love you?" even if that someone is you.

Even piety provides no guarantee. Pecola was pious. She prayed:

> Each night, without fail, she prayed for blue eyes. Fervently, for a year, she had prayed. Although somewhat discouraged, she was not without hope. To have something as wonderful as that happen would take a long time (p. 40).

Even the church at times acts as a collaborator with the rhinoceros. Here the image of the priest in the story makes clear the folly of some black preachers. When Pecola asks the priest, Elihue Micah Whitcomb, to change her eyes he ruminates that "he thought that it was at once the most fantastic and the most logical petition he had ever received. Here was an ugly little girl asking for beauty" (p. 137).

Like the tailors in the story of the Emperor's new clothes, he tells her that she, in fact, now has blue eyes, visible to those who have real sight.

The rhinoceros in this story wins. Pecola had to come to terms with marginality or go mad, and she decides for the latter. The priest blesses her choice. "So it was . . . A little black girl yearns for the blue eyes of a little white girl, and the horror at the heart of her yearning is exceeded only by the evil of fulfillment" (p. 158).

However, her choice does not bring her to the white world. She remains on the edge. She remains marginal. Not only does the outdoor marginality effect a sense of self and property, but it also informs a sense of sexuality. Pecola's last name was Breedlove, though her family breeds no love. What they do breed is sexual violence. Pecola is sexually abused by her father, and she becomes pregnant from this act of incest. Now, she is alienated from the black community in a special way. We all have a bit of Pecola in us where the rhinoceros tries to overcome our better selves. Pecola's madness threatens each black person just as the serpent tempts Eve and just as the sin is couching at the door ready to consume Cain. The tragedy of Pecola comes from her abandonment to the temptation.

Our fear of the rhinoceros is so potent that we avoid those who succumb too fully. "So we avoided Pecola Breedlove—forever" (p. 158).

When we can not tame the rhinoceros we find refuge in madness. When we cannot come to grips with marginality, we create an imaginary world of our own. "She [Pecola], however, stepped into madness, a madness which protected her from us simply because it bored us in the end" (p. 159).

Nonetheless, we root for Pecola to make the better choice, to come to grips with marginality. Claudia explains eloquently:

There is more at stake than the child, Pecola, and her

unborn baby. The moral order and the environment are at stake. Just as Cain's murder was the ground crying, so also the ground weeps for Pecola and refuses to bear flowers in the mean season. "Quiet as it's kept, there were no marigolds in the fall of 1941. We thought, that it was because Pecola was having her father's baby that the marigolds did not grow" (p 9).

Nonetheless, the locus of blame lies outside of Pecola. The end of the novel begins with the juxtaposition of Pecola and the marigolds that do not bear fruit. The marigolds never appear and Pecola's baby dies.

A Critical Reading of Genesis 3–4

The Yahwist pulled together both the story of creation (Gen. 2:4b-28) as well as the story of the garden and Cain and Abel (Gen. 3:1–4:26). However, in Gen. 3–4 the Yahwist depict the patriarchal world of the United Monarchy as being a given reality from God. The liberation tone of Gen. 2 vanishes completely.

Gen. 3–4 recounts the erosion of partnership. The intervention of the "other" provided the corrosive element in this erosion. The appropriate vulnerability, depicted by the nudity in Gen. 2, gives way to shame in vulnerability. The self-hate generated in these stories makes cooperation and partnership the exception, not the rule. The intervention logically and literally precedes the loss of partnership. Intimacy evaporates before the heat of the "other's" lies. Chapter 3 is divided into three parts: (1) the temptation or intervention (Gen. 3:1-5); (2) the act of disobedience (Gen. 3:6); and, (3) the result (Gen. 3:7-24). The third section recounts how the first lovers, Adam and Eve, lost three intimate relationships. Thus, the story provides for us a model of broken partnership.

The intervention begins with the description of the serpent. The serpent was the most subtle of creatures (v. 1a). The serpent whispers to the woman (v. 1b), beginning with an exaggeration. God had instructed the man and the woman not to eat from the tree of the knowledge of good and evil, but all the other trees in the garden were at their disposal. The serpent lied, telling them they could eat from the special tree. The story begins with the deception.

The woman corrects the misinterpretation of the serpent (Gen. 3:2-3). The serpent does not hesitate; it contradicts the woman's information. Then it proposes that God lied and that, further, God knows the lie in the instructions given to the man and the woman (v. 5).

The second part of the chapter describes the act of disobedience. This section is the smallest in the chapter (v. 6). The writer frames the act as rational. The woman acts because the fruit strikes her as attractive and as a desired commodity. Her actions are prudent.

The third section describes the results of the prudent act. Disaster results from this "rational" action. First, they lose the symbol of appropriate vulnerability when their nudity becomes a source of shame to them. They lose access to one another as naked lovers. Now they meet through the fig leaf aprons they fashioned for themselves.

Next, they flee from the presence of God. When God catches them, they say, "I was afraid because I was naked; and I hid myself." (v. 10). The sign of their vulnerability now looms as a source of fear. This prompts a bout of blaming others for the act (vv. 12-13). The man blames the woman ("that woman, she . . ."), but the woman is God's creation; so the man implicitly blames God as well.

God's response to the blaming is swift. The whole creation suffers from this act. Alienation becomes the new norm (vv. 14-24). From that point forward, the partnership of women and men becomes a miracle. Partnership breaks with conventional wisdom. It becomes strained. The partnership between the human community and the land likewise becomes combative.

Cain was the first criminal. His act of fratricide may be a helpful model in understanding the nature of black on black crime. Cain violates the three key relationships. His crime is against a person, his brother Abel, against God, and he causes the land to participate in the crime as an innocent witness.

The United Monarchy constitutes the historical context for this chapter. The background of Solomon and David shows through time and time again. For instance, one notices that Cain is the older brother. A recurring theme in the material of the Yahwist, David's theologian, was to explain why David and his son Solomon ascend to the throne despite the fact that they were not the eldest sons. The Yahwist, therefore, depict the eldest son as a villain. This is evident in the Joseph story also.

There are other elements of class conflict in the story. The writer describes Abel as a shepherd and Cain as a farmer (Gen. 4:2b). Here, the conflict between the shepherd and the farmer is born. These elements demonstrate the structural elements that contribute to the description of Cain. His birth order and occupation offended the agenda of the king's storyteller. But Cain is merely the representative of a group of people. The Yahwist wishes to limit the power of that group.

The brothers brought their offerings before God, and God preferred Abel's sacrifice. While commentators feel obliged to explain why God made such a choice, the biblical text does not explain God's decision. The audience of ancient Israel would understand how wheat, oats and barley would compare with a sacrifice of barbecue for us. The parallel can be found in the Jacob/Esau story, where the wild game became the delicacy on which the inheritance hung (Gen. 27).

Anger consumed Cain, "his countenance fell" (Gen. 4:5b), because his offering was not accepted. The writer describes God as a self-indulgent king. God says to Cain:

"Why are you angry, and why has your countenance fallen?" If you do well, will you not be accepted?" (Gen. 4:6).

The answer to this question resounds in the breast of black women and men across this nation. NO! Cain could say, "I will not be acceptable." No matter where you teach, no matter how much money you make, you cannot make a woman into a man and you can't make a person of color into a white person. We can never be acceptable.

Structurally, given the agenda of the Yahwist, there was no chance that Cain would succeed. He was an eldest son in the court of the younger son. He was a farmer in the jurisdiction of shepherds.

The storyteller has masterfully made a victim the criminal. Once again, we should note that the structural issues remain even in the blocks to interpersonal partnership. Black biblical hermeneutics must find the structural issues in scripture as well as those in contemporary black experience.

The self-indulgent king, using the language of God continues in 4:7b: "And if you do not do well, sin is crouching at the door; its desire is for you, but you must master it." Cain will not do well. A spiral of death captures Cain. He is structurally locked into "not doing well." Thereby sin waits at the door to devour Cain.

The challenge that Cain must confront, the temptation to sin, falls poignantly on the ears of black people. The reader must be aware that the mastering of sin means the acceptance of the capricious acceptance of one's sacrifices. We remember that there is no reason given for God's decision. The task before Cain is to accept God's decision no matter how frivolous it may be. Cain should be a good "slave." The structural issues of class and occupation demonstrate a blocked partnership between God and Cain.

The story does not move on the structural issues. Cain

goes into the field with his brother and kills him. As we look at this story with new eyes, we see that this event, is tragic and unseasoned. Nonetheless, the partnership of brothers is irrevocably blocked through this act.

An example from life might be instructive. As a father I occasionally have to punish my children. I am a good bit bigger than they are and am seen as being more powerful than they. Seldom do my children lash out at me in retaliation. However, it is not unusual that after one is reprimanded he will go and hit his brother.

The self-indulgent king in the guise of God has mistreated Cain. Now Cain attacks the innocent Abel. What better analogy is there for black on black crime? When you cannot effectively victimize those who structurally keep you out, then you victimize those close at hand.

God now returns. God requests of Cain information about his partner and brother, Abel. Cain's response is, "I do not know, am I my brother's keeper?" The Hebrew for "keeper" [samar] means "to keep" as in "to protect. A dynamic translation of Cain's answer might be, "Am I my brother's protector and partner?"

Cain's rhetorical question has immense power. The audience knows from its training in the home that the answer is "Yes!" This is the nature of the person to person partnership, now broken. When the affirmation that forms the bedrock of a community becomes a trite question, our response parallels that described of God in this instance: "What have you done?" The absence of unity and partnership constitutes the loss of land, community, and God. Cain, what have you done?

The black-on-black crime is more than a class phenomenon. The black middle class everyday asks Cain's question, "Am I my brother and sister's protector?" For a black biblical hermeneutic, the answer must be a resounding "Yes!" time and time again. This represents a major challenge for the black middle class.

Christian tradition has made the point at times that the mark of Cain was being black. The black poet Phyllis Wheatley powerfully describes this in her poem, "Black as Cain." It misses the point to maintain that Cain was turned black as a punishment for the murder of his brother (Gen. 4:11-15). We know that this is ludicrous. The mark of Cain was to be a sign that persons should not execute violence on his person (Gen. 4:15). It was a protection against violence being committed against him. A person's being black in America has seldom been a reason for white people to eschew violence, lest they stir the wrath of God because of this biblical injunction. On the contrary, being black in this country has been a implicit permission to commit acts of violence against black people.

The interpretation that Cain was turned black is wrong for another reason. Cain was functionally black from the beginning of the story. As Cain was structurally kept out of the program of success, by his birth order and occupation, he experienced a key element of black experience. Politically he was black.

However, he made a mistake. Cain responded to the structural issues of his social position with violence against his sibling. Cain took the "power as coercion" model as his own. However, he did not have the ability to coerce the structural realities. So he coerced one like himself, his brother in this case. An empowerment model would ask whether Cain should not make a pact with Abel to boycott this capricious God.

Andrew Young tells the story about a peaceful demonstration that was broken up by the violence of the police. The demonstrators returned to the church headquarters. There was a sense that they wanted to abandon the strategy of non-violence. Rather than protest against this feeling, the leaders asked the people specifically what they were going to bring to the battle. One said a shotgun; another had a .38 caliber; another had a .45 caliber pistol. As the community heard one another describe their weapons, a sense of reason overcame the group. They did not have enough weapons of coercion to fight bullets with bullets. Unity and partnership revolve around empowerment, not power as coercion. Furthermore, empowerment represents not only the morally superior position but also the more successful alternative for the black community.

UNITY IN CHRIST: THE RHINOCEROS TAMER The "other" or *daimon* acts to break the unity of creation. All the kings horses and all the kings men can not put it together again. But the event of the Christ can. The material in Gen. 3-4 gives us a picture of how the rhinoceros of racism tramples the lives of black women and men. Only Christ can tame the rhinoceros.

The reality of black existence breaks the unity of life. The unity of life requires the intervention of the "other." The "other" provides an avenue for black women and men to return to unity. We see this in persons but also in the model *par excellence* of the Christ event.

Black church tradition represents the unity of creation, but the unity of creation experienced in the black church constitutes a broken unity. The egg is broken but it can be put back together with the help of the "other".

Recovery of the Biblical Tradition

The title of Alice Walker's novel, *The Third Life of Grange Copeland*, makes clear the importance of the *daimon*. Grange Copeland, the main character in the novel, had three lives: Grange had his own life, that of his son Brownfield [son], and the life of his granddaughter Ruth.

Ruth, the *daimon* saves Grange Copeland. Grange misspent his own youth, and later deserted his wife and family. His response to racism germinates in silence and blooms in violence and isolation. Brownfield, Grange Copeland's son, learns rejection when his father leaves, and, again, when his mother commits suicide, leaving Brownfield alone. So Brownfield sets off to find his father; instead, he finds the madame that his father has lived with for a time. He becomes her lover partly as a way to connect with his father.

Brownfield later marries and reproduces the destructive relationship with his wife that his father had had with Brownfield's mother. Brownfield's wife tries to respond to the unrelenting physical violence of their relationship. She obtains a short respite when she is able to exercise enough power to hold back Brownfield's violence. However, her valiant effort comes to nothing. Brownfield waits, and murders her eventually.

Brownfield's brutality does not end with his wife. He brutalizes his daughters. He calls his daughters whores, and this label becomes a self-fulfilling prophecy. After their mother's death, the daughters, with the exception of Ruth, are sent away and become prostitutes.

Ruth alone escapes, and her escape is the third life of Grange Copeland. She is the *daimon* in the novel. She does not appear miraculously the way the messenger in Gen. 32 does. However, the way she penetrates Grange Copeland's affection is just as miraculous.

Brownfield finds only hate when he sees the affection Grange has for Ruth. He tries to get custody of Ruth, but Grange has to prevent this. Brownfield's hate will only destroy Ruth as it did his wife and other daughters. Brownfield's violence would destroy Ruth as surely as Grange's distance destroyed Brownfield.

The resolution springs from the confrontation of Grange and Brownfield before the white judge. The whites in this southern city, as in many others—South or North—were unable to see the human factors at work in the situation of blacks. They simply saw color. They act with the most insidious cruelty. Ignorance of black life, coupled with the power of Jim Crow society, is the cruelest joke God could play on the black community. The white judge awards custody of Ruth to her father. In the context of the irrationality of white so-called justice, it falls to Grange to protect Ruth any way he can. So, he kills Brownfield.

The result of circumventing the irrational white justice by black folks means death or prison. Grange could have incriminated his son, but to do so in a white courtroom was unacceptable.

The protection of Ruth cost Grange his life. On the other hand, the willingness to give up his life for her was the witness to his life. The healing came from change. The death of Grange Copeland gives witness to the healing change that transforms.

A Critical Reading of Gen. 32

The life of Jacob witnesses to the brokenness of human life. The story (Gen. 32:22-32) describes him before the ford of the Jabbok river. After sending his family with their possessions across the river, he waits for Esau.

This passage reveals a theophany, the description of an appearance of God. The encounter between Jacob and God illustrates the nature of the encounter between God and black people in America. Three themes surface: aloneness, wrestling, and blessing.

Aloneness. Jacob remains on the bank of the Jabbok alone. The Hebrew accents the passive, that Jacob was left alone. There is no family or company to support him as he wrestles with God.

Wrestling. An angel wrestles with Jacob. The Hebrew term for wrestle does not appear anywhere else in scripture. Nonetheless it is clear that the two struggle, not with the elegance of olympic wrestlers or professional

45

boxers, but, rather, like middle-aged men tussling in the streets.

For black people, living in white America provides two choices: wrestling or social death. The results of this wrestling match do not surprise the black community. The angel touches the hollow of Jacob's thigh and dislocates it. For those black people who decide to wrestle instead of die, it should be known that there remains a price for wrestling. No black child born in the United States goes to his or her grave whole. The wrestling snatches from every one of them an arm or a thigh, and from another, a piece of his or her soul.

Blessing. At the break of day the angel asks to be released. Only a blessing will cause Jacob to relent. So the angel changes Jacob's name. Just as the wrestling takes a part of Jacob, so also the blessing changes him in another way. They stand as parallel tracks. Those who do not wrestle abdicate their blessing, but not all those who wrestle will be blessed.

Jacob persists. That sets him apart in this story. Black people must not only wrestle, but must also persist. The blessing goes to those who continue to struggle.

The blessing consists of a name change. The idea of name changes is not new for the black community. Sojourner Truth was not born with that name; she had another name when she was a slave, a name intentionally discarded with her slave identity. The changing of the name is part of black church tradition. The old Negro spiritual makes the point: "I've got a new name, way over in Zion! It's mine. I declare it's mine." Name-changing was an act of blessing and liberation.

The black community also knows of the changing of names as oppression. Black slaves and immigrants of all kinds were stripped of their original names and given the names of their masters, socially acceptable names. In

Alex Haley's *Roots,* Kunta Kinte gives way to Toby. But the master's word is not the last word.

The Black Muslim tradition sparked a resurgence in naming for liberation. There were a number of name changes that captured the attention of the American public in the second half of the twentieth century. Cassius Clay, the world heavyweight boxing champion, became Mohammed Ali. Lew Alcindor of basketball fame became Karem Abdul Jabbar. These name changes were, on the face of it, personal choices. At the same time, they were witnesses to a deeper political and spiritual awareness. Nowhere is this more clearly evident than in the name change of Malcolm Little to Malcolm X.

The changing of one's name is a tradition that is seen in biblical tradition as well as in black church tradition. We remember immediately the changing of Abram and Sarai to Abraham and Sarah (Gen. 17). We are reminded of Saul who became Paul (Acts 9). We know that Jacob's name was changed to Israel (Gen. 32). These texts accent the discontinuity between the person and his previous identity. It should be noted that the Abraham and Jacob traditions refer to corporate realities. The changing of the name was the changing of identity for political reasons.

The name change tells us about the "other" with whom we wrestle. The "other" or *daimon* can be the rhinoceros of racism and internalized self-hate. The *daimon* or "other" can also be the one who redeems us from broken unity, as with Jacob.

Jesus the Christ, the rhinoceros tamer, redeems us for unity and partnership. Jesus represents the God who changes our names. This is paralleled with the words of the spiritual: "I told Jesus, it would be all right, if He changed my name." This song points to the social power of name-changing, as well.

These accent the discontinuity between the previous life and the new life in community. Black church

47

tradition picks up on this in the interpretation of scripture. The slave experience made such an interpretive device necessary. It could be said that the immigrant experience works in a similar way. However, the stigma of discontinuity in the slave experience has a profound effect on the interpretive strategy.

The black church is the church of Jesus Christ. Nothing is more consistent in black churches than the centrality of the figure of Jesus as the Christ. The christology of the black church does not move from a particular text. Black church christology springs from the soil of black suffering.

From the red clay of Georgia to the black asphalt of Watts, the ground of black suffering ever cries out, "slavery!" The institution and experience of slavery and its inheritance stands as a symbol of the obstacles to partnership and unity. Racism remains the rhinoceros before our eyes. Christ, the name-changer and the rhinoceros-tamer, requires a different christology.

Slavery redefines the two christological positions, *imitatio christi* and *christus victor*. These two positions usually work together in a Christian community. Most reflections on Christian ethics and theology include one as primary and the other as secondary. The black church accents *christus victor*. Black hymnody and liturgics demonstrate the centrality of the victorious Christ, the one who changes our names. We shall be vindicated!

> He's my rock, my sword, my shield
> He's my wheel in the middle of a wheel.

The *imitatio christi*, for the black church, constitutes a given, not a selection. Moses came forth in the midst of oppression. Christ, likewise came forth into oppression. Oppression constitutes a given for a Christ figure. Like the Christ, the black Christian—the disinherited—comes forth into oppression. We imitate Christ at that point whether we, as black Christians, want to or not.

On the other hand, *imitatio christi* stands in opposition to the imitation of the rhinoceros of racism. As we strive to be more like Claudia and less like Pecola, we are actively involved in the imitation of Christ. As we say no to the internalization of racism, we imitate the Christ. As we seek freedom and justice, we imitate Christ. As we wrestle against principalities and powers, we imitate Christ.

Thus, we see the centrality of Christ in the black church. The hiss of the whip on the back of black men, and the tears of the women stripped bare before the auction block generate black christology. Christ gives us names of freedom while we yet remain in the house of bondage. The Christ proclaims our victory over the rhinoceros and provides a model to counter the culture's racial rhinoceros.

No text tradition in the New Testament generates the black church position with regard to christology or, for that matter, Christian ethics. Jesus Christ represents the interpretative key, but the New Testament does not constitute the major biblical text. Christ represents the reconciling forces of the divine. Through Jesus the Christ, unity and partnership are redeemed.

Ruth represents a Christ figure: she redeems Grange from a life of self-hate and violence. At the same time, Grange is a Christ figure: he gives up his life to save Ruth from the sociopathic Brownfield. In this regard, both Ruth and Grange illustrate the way that persons in the black community imitate the redemption we find in Christ, albeit in small ways.

Black fiction, like the black experience it recreates, describes a world of fragile partnerships between black women and men. One need only read Alice Walker's novel *The Color Purple* to see the fragility of partnerships between black women and men. The same theme dominates Toni Morrison's *Tar Baby*.

Unity and models of partnership in the black community fight a never-ending battle against the ghost of the slavemasters, living and dead. At the close of Lorraine Hansberry's play, "Raisin in the Sun," the character Mama says about her oldest son: "He finally come into his manhood today, didn't he? Kind of like a rainbow after a rain. . . ." This hopeful ending to the play encourages black people to continue the struggle. However, it does not mean that every rain has a rainbow or that every man or woman comes into his or her own sense of strength in vulnerability. The challenge for intimacy between black women and men looms large, on the one hand; on the other hand, the issue of black-on-black violence presents a related challenge. The statistics of black on black crime stagger the imagination. The situation compels the black church to answer with an explanation as well as a strategy.

Black-on-black crime and the drug-related killings in cities and towns constitute a residual effect of blocked interpersonal partnership. Interpersonal blocks to partnership cannot be separated from such matters as structural poverty and racism. In fact, structural poverty and racism become the seedbed, the origin of interpersonal blocks to partnership.

However, the root of blocks to partnership should not be attributed to all of these externals. The origin of blocks to interpersonal partnership begins with the criminal. The perpetrator of the violence interprets the structural issues in such a way as to misapprehend the nature of power. Violence defines power. Such a definition orders the world of the criminal and effectively blocks interpersonal partnership, which develops from inappropriate vulnerability, not violence.

Violence uses power for coercion. Appropriate vulnerability engenders empowerment of the partners. Power becomes part of a zero sum game, in which a gain for one must inexorably result in loss for another or others.

The strategy to meet black-on-black crime begins with a new concept of power. The rubric of appropriate vulnerability moves the game from competition and its concomitant violence to a model of appropriate vulnerability and empowerment.

The Exodus tradition (Gen. 37–Josh. 24) represents the central text for the black church. The slave experience, understood christologically, represents the interpretive key for that tradition. All subsequent biblical reflection moves from these two building blocks of content. Just as it moves from the three notes of recovery of tradition, critical reading of texts, and application. However, the black church tenaciously holds on to the power of the Christ to reconcile the world. The unity and partnership fall on us afresh through the Christ event.

Chapter IV

Patriotism and Loyalty

The Foundation of a Quest for Black Liberation

Through Christ the black church can attain unity and partnership; however, this demands an interpretation of the slave experience. The three elements of Sojourner Truth's life—preacher, slave, and abolitionist—speaks to the unity of life. Creation and christology give witness to this unity in partnership. However, the absurdity of the slave experience in this context demands explication.

Black church tradition interprets the slave experience through a new reading of the Exodus tradition. The slave experience describes a broken loyalty. Unlike the white indentured servants who could eventually find freedom and justice, the slave experience left blacks in the United States permanently labelled as slaves, people who could never seem to find justice and freedom in the United States. Because of racism, the worker, never finds humanizing loyal reward for labor.

The black community stands committed to the values of freedom espoused by the framers of the constitution without accepting their racism. The patriotism of black people takes root in the interpretation of the Exodus tradition as a precursor to the experience of black people in America.

What do we mean by *patriotism?* For the black community, patriotism refers to loyalty to a nation and the ideals that a nation holds inviolate, such as freedom and justice. Patriotism can never mean blind faith in policies that violate the tenets of a nation's ability to preserve itself.

Black patriotism moves from this perspective. No one should be surprised, then, when we recall the acceptance speech of Martin Luther King, Jr., when he received the Nobel Peace Prize. "I accept this award today with an abiding faith in America and an audacious faith in the future of mankind."[1]

Loyalty involves decisions for and against something else. Pharaoh's loyalty lay with the oppressive economic system. In the case of blacks in America, that also means racism. Nonetheless, the economic dimensions of the issue remain. In order to remain faithful to the system, Pharaoh became disloyal to his workers, the Hebrew slaves. The breech means that loyalty to the leadership of the nation and patriotism no longer go hand in hand.

Patriotism runs deep in the veins of the sons and daughters of slaves. Loyalty to the American system represents an *a priori* in traditional theology of the black church.[2] Nonetheless, blacks have consistently been recipients of a broken loyalty as blacks and as workers.

The Exodus tradition illustrates the conflict between the symbol of the oppression, Pharaoh, and the symbol of liberation, God. Patriotism and loyalty find their measure in relationship to the God of freedom. The term *'abed,* translated as "serve," also means "worship." The double meaning of this word points to the tension in patriotism. The powers of the oppressive system demand the "service" that should be reserved for God. The Exodus tradition depicts the Hebrews as choosing between

Pharaoh and God time and time again. While there is black patriotism in the United States, the challenge for the black church remains the relationship with God, who brought us out of bondage. The black church today, in its use of scripture and its life in general, chooses between a system and God.

The Exodus tradition interpreting the slave experience represents an expanse of texts. The miracle at the Reed Sea[3] presents only one element of the tradition. This chapter outlines the Exodus tradition in black church tradition. The story begins with the explanation of how the Hebrews got to Egypt. It concludes with the conquest of the Promised Land and the covenant with the God of freedom.

The Exodus Tradition in Black Spirituals

In the previous chapter, we saw how black literary tradition could illustrate the interpretation of scripture in the black community. Here we shall see how the spirituals represent black biblical tradition.

STYLE AND CONTENT The song, "Go Down, Moses" explicates the Exodus tradition for the black and slave church. The analysis of the song indicates the style of black biblical interpretation and the content of the Exodus tradition, according to black church tradition. This African spiritual has many more verses than are usually seen in print.[4]

The song combines a code song[5] and midrash. The weaving of these two elements sets a tone for all subsequent biblical exegesis in the black church. This combination clearly marks the style of black biblical interpretation. Code songs conveyed information between slaves that the masters could not decipher. Scholars like John Lovell and James Cone have perceived the vital role of social protest in the spirituals through the code songs.[6]

Midrash interprets scripture in a homiletical fashion for each new generation. In the midrashic world the text represents an inexhaustible source of meaning.[7] The challenges of the life of the believing community find answers in the biblical text for those preachers who can tap it.

We notice that the forms of interpretation in the song "Go Down, Moses" illustrates an essential element in black biblical interpretation. The combination of midrash and code song points to the unity of social action and reflection on biblical text in the black community. For the black community midrash involves a political reflection.

The content of the Exodus tradition is expansive according to the writer of the song. The song begins, "When Israel was in Egypt land." This represents the Joseph story (Gen. 37-48) through the story of the Hebrew slaves (Exod. 1-2). However, the writer makes the point that the story moves from the Exodus event (Exod. 14-15) through the conquest of the Promised Land (Josh. 6). Finally, the story concludes with the role of the Christ in the liberation process in the words of the spiritual, "O, let us all from bondage flee . . . And let us all in Christ be free."

This understanding of history permeates black church historiography. The rise of the slave church represents the period in Egypt. The black church of reconstruction and Jim Crow represent the wilderness wandering stage. The conquest and the struggle between Satan and the Christ represent the Civil Rights era to the present. This historiography is so central that even theologians like James Cone still find it persuasive.[8]

How this historiographic template develops in the song "Go Down, Moses" explains the connection between the

56

Exodus event and the larger Exodus tradition, which includes the taking of the land. Notice, for instance, the lines:

> Jordan shall stand up like a wall . . .
> And the walls of Jericho shall fall.

The connection between the miracle at the reed sea (Exod. 14) and the miraculous capture of Jericho (Josh. 6) gives witness to a horizon of freedom, not a single event. A subsequent verse echoes a similar theme:

> Your foes shall not before you stand . . .
> And you'll possess fair Canaan's land . . .

The writer connects the escape with the establishment of the people. They escape the oppressive situation, but there is something much more. God propels them from the escape into a time of economic stability. It is almost as if there is an implicit social statement that freedom does not exist without economic stability.

A story of salvation history in black church tradition must have a reference to the Christ. Freedom takes root in the Christ event:

> O let us from all bondage flee . . .
> And let us all in Christ be free . . .

The redemption of the political realm requires a connection with Jesus Christ in black church tradition.

The song divides history into three parts. The first part begins with Israel in Egypt; the second describes the action from Pharaoh's confrontation through the conquest of the Promised Land. This section of scripture explains how the believing community got out of Egypt and into the Promised Land. The third part describes the confrontation between Christ and Satan.

Critical Reading of the Exodus Tradition

On the one hand, the story in "Go Down, Moses" could be characterized as: how we got in; how we got out; and how we got over. "When Israel was in Egypt's land," describes life in the house of bondage. "As Israel stood by the water side," describes how we got out. "And let us all in Christ be free," describes how we got over then and now.

This outline of salvation history represents an essential building block in the theology of the marginalized. This theology of a people on the edge—included, but excluded—frames black patriotism and the process conforms to the elements of the Exodus tradition.

What does the theology of the marginalized mean? The marginalized of a society are those persons who, because of their functions, psychologically or economically, provide such a service that they cannot be dispensed with. At the same time, these persons are structurally separated from the exercise of political, economic and cultural power by the dominant group. Nonetheless, these people have theological formulations, which are the spiritual reflections and ruminations of the excluded, the theology of the marginalized.

Black people in America are marginalized. We provide a range of services for white America, economically, psychologically, and otherwise. Therefore, the expulsion of black people from the face of the continent is not desired, and the violence against black people in this culture does not move to total genocide.

WHEN ISRAEL WAS IN EGYPT LAND . . .This part of the tradition has two parts. The first part is often forgotten, the role of Joseph in the Exodus tradition. Joseph is more than a literary device to get the Hebrews into Egypt (Gen. 37-48); he contrasts the values of the Egyptians with those of the Hebrews. The second part describes the resistance of the Hebrew midwives and the follies of leadership not grounded in a basic religious experience (Exod. 1-6).

The Joseph story really contains two separate, but related, stories. The first story is of Joseph the loyal worker. The second story recounts the struggle for loyalty between brothers. The combination of these two stories provides a foundation for a theology for the marginalized.

Joseph provides more than a literary connection between the Genesis material and the Exodus tradition; the depiction contrasts Joseph the loyal worker to the Egyptians.

On the face of it, the story of Potiphar's wife recounts a simple tale. Potiphar buys Joseph. Potiphar's wife finds Joseph attractive. She tries to seduce him, but fails. At that point, she accuses him of attempted rape. Subsequently, Potiphar has Joseph imprisoned for his alleged crime (Gen. 39).

Typically, many interpreters of this passage have arrived at misogynist conclusions: the woman, Potiphar's wife, accuses the innocent man, Joseph. The moral of the story becomes that women will falsely accuse men of attempted rape.

Black interpretation of this passage does not deny the patriarchal and misogynist elements in this tale, but it focuses on the political elements, noting that the story is about the decadent Egyptians. The story accents the loyalty of Joseph by contrasting him to Potiphar's wife. It also depicts the Egyptians as being not only oppressive, but stupid as well.

Philo (20 B.C.E.–50 C.E.), a Jewish philosopher, tried to explain the subjugation of the Hebrews by the Egyptians. He maintained that the Egyptians were a "voluptuous people." This term, not our usual connotation, refers to people devoted to luxury, elegance, the pleasure of the senses, good looks, and the good life. In other words, *cosmetic beauty* which must be maintained at any cost, no matter what support system has to be maintained at any cost, no matter what support system has to be developed to maintain it. It also suggests that "voluptuous people" don't dirty their hands or work at things that might spoil the looks or break the fingernails or muss the hair or make-up or rumple the clothing. Consequently, manual labor had to be contracted out to slaves to maintain the "voluptuous people."

What is at stake here is a critique of a type of economy. Throughout the biblical period, Egypt represented the center of oppression. The economic model of ancient Egypt contradicted the egalitarian tendencies in Israelite religion. The pyramids and the monumental architecture stood as a monument to a redistribution economy, which took goods and services from the poor of the land and used them for the benefit of the wealthy of the land, usually the king. While this breaks our anticipations conditioned by modern economic language, nonetheless, such a model adequately describes many ancient economies.

The lifestyle of the royal court emerges from this type of economy. The voluptuous nature, the sheer decadence, and the economic structure of the Egyptian society made the slavery of the Hebrews, or some other group, inevitable. Potiphar's wife embodies the excesses of the redistribution economy as seen through the eyes of the Hebrews.

Joseph embodies, on the other hand, the loyal servant. He worked for one of the king's guards, Potiphar. The story of Potiphar's wife frames Joseph's loyalty to his Egyptian masters. This tale contrasts his loyalty to the disloyalty of Potiphar's wife. Further, it contrasts Joseph's loyalty to his owner and the owner's lack of trust and subsequent disloyalty to Joseph.

To our way of thinking, a wife should embody the

maximum loyalty. Joseph, on the other hand, should constitute the minimal loyalty to his master, Potiphar. However, it was Joseph, not Potiphar's wife, who maintained Potiphar's interests.

Throughout the story there is the juxtaposition of luxury and loyalty. Amidst the luxury of this decadent people, Joseph finds himself in prison. However, the loyalty of Joseph is only exceeded by the loyalty of God. Even in prison, the presence of God dominates the context. God's power and Joseph's resilience shines through.

The resilience of Joseph, who represents the marginalized community, stems from the power of God. Even in prison he had visions (Gen. 40). Here we find a recurring theme in the Exod tradition: a gospel of liberation always demonstrates and proclaims God's ability to make a way out of no way. Therefore, even in the midst of prison God's revelation was there for Joseph. The theme of God's loyalty is wrapped up with the theme of God's power.

Loyalty between marginalized people. The rest of the Joseph novella revolves around the reconciliation between Joseph and his Hebrew brothers. A morality tale emerges about the relationship between the powerful brother within the political system and the powerless brothers outside the system. One could easily make the connection between the black middle and black poor class. The theme of the story reflects more than what happens within one group of siblings; it reflects the interaction of black persons with one another.

Chapters 30–41 and 47:13-26 depict the loyalty of Joseph to the Egyptians. Gen. 37 and 42-47:12 describe the reconciliation between Joseph and his brothers. The description of broken loyalty that transforms into filial solidarity parallels the loyalty theme in the rest of the Joseph material. There is, on the one hand, solidarity with one's brothers and sisters, which always needs to be reconciled. At the same time, there is the loyalty to the Egyptians, or whatever the local economy may be at the time.

We could ask how black women and men could sell their brothers and sisters into slavery in Egypt? The black middle class benefits from the plight of the working poor, often without any thought to the cost to those poorer black brothers and sisters. There are other parallels that one might constructively draw where one group or class benefits from another group having less.

We could ask how black men and women can re-establish loyalty to their black brothers and sisters. The story of Joseph reminds us that we share the circumstance of being marginalized. Further, like Joseph and his brothers, the black poor and the black middle class can forge a newly invigorated solidarity. As a theology for the marginalized takes practical shape, such solidarity is a necessity.

Resistance in the Slave Church. Exod. 1–2 describe the experience of the slave church in Egypt. The narrative consists of three elements: the story of the wise Hebrew midwives; the story of the birth of Moses; and the story of Moses' attempt at revolution. The themes that surface are the power of God and the cunning of the Hebrew slaves.

The first story (Exod. 1) describes the wisdom of the Hebrew midwives and the folly of Pharaoh. The Hebrew slave, represented by the Hebrew midwives, remains resourceful even in the oppression in Egypt. Women act as the hands of God in this chapter. The women are given instructions from Pharaoh that they were to kill every male child at birth. But the midwives feared the LORD (Exod. 1:17). Therefore, they did not comply with the Pharaoh's orders. The fear of the LORD becomes a reason for the loyalty to God as well as for the awareness of God as the ultimate power even in the midst of the Egyptian social system. The midwives' loyalty to the LORD superseded any loyalty to Pharaoh or the system he represented.

Pharaoh confronts the women for not carrying out his instructions. They argue that the Hebrew women are not like Egyptian women. The Hebrews are vigorous in their childbirth (Exod. 1:19). Here we see an ethnic slur against the Egyptians, and this deception indicates the cunning of the Hebrews. (The combination of loyalty and cunning are stock in trade for the Hebrews.) These women subverted Pharaoh's machine of death.

Again, women act as the hands of God in this story of salvation history. Moses' mother and his sister, Miriam, display cunning and loyalty. Compassion fills out the picture of this group of slave women. His mother saw that Moses was a godly child. Her compassion for Moses is not simply that he is her child, but a perception of his connection with God. Thus, connecting compassion with piety.

Also in this story we find irony. The mother hides the child with the help of her daughter. Pharaoh had ordered that the male children be cast into the Nile to drown (Exod. 1:22). Now, Pharaoh's daughter pulls Moses' basket out of the Nile. Miriam oversees the entire scene. She maneuvers events so her mother is paid to be the nanny of her baby brother, the new possession of Pharaoh's daughter (Exod. 2:9-10). The irony is threefold: Women dominate the story of the birth of Moses; Pharaoh's daughter saves Moses; and Moses' biological mother becomes his nurse.

The third story picks up the action sometime later when Moses is an adult. The themes of loyalty and cunning give way to an apology for the need to blend radicalism with piety or religious experience. Moses' attempt at radicalism could not succeed because liberation only follows after the religious experience with God at the burning bush (Exod. 3).

We have no biblical stories about the young boy Moses. Characteristic of youth, he tries to put a puzzle together before he has all the pieces. Moses tries radicalism before he has the religious experience and piety.

The tradition of black radicalism finds roots in the Exodus tradition. God worked through the midwives and Moses' mother as God worked through other women like Sojourner Truth, Harriet Tubman, and Fannie Lou Hammer. But black radicalism parallels black pietism. God's loyalty through people parallels God's loyalty through religious experience. That is the foundation of black piety. Black radicalism is inextricably tied to black religious experience.

The description of Moses' efforts for justice prior to his religious experience can not work. Moses' attempt at radicalism failed. Moses went out and saw injustice. Moses killed an Egyptian, and this act resulted in recriminations. Moses did not build solidarity with the Hebrews with this act. The next day the Hebrews ask whether Moses will kill them as he had the Egyptian (Exod. 2:14). Pharaoh sought to kill Moses for his crime, so Moses fled (Exod. 2:15). Without the basis in piety and religious experience, radicalism leads to alienation, not liberation.

The Hebrews cried out to God (Exod. 2:23-24). God saw, remembered, and assured them that their God knew their condition. The result had to be liberation. The context of this liberation was not merely radicalism, since radicalism alone had failed. Pietism and religious experience, calling on God, constitute the essential ingredients for their liberation.

Pietism in the Slave Church. The presence of God empowers the radicalism. Pietism complements radicalism. The place of Exod. 3 in the Exodus tradition makes this point clear. Pietism and radicalism form the body of the promise (Exod. 3:17-22), that God will support the Hebrews and that God will validate the appropriateness of their loyalty. They will move from slavery to self-sufficiency.

This primary religious experience took place in the wilderness. The Hebrew term *midbar* refers to the place of revelation, apostasy, and possible death. The wilderness represents the place of crisis and opportunity. For black slaves, the experience in America represents the wilderness.

Moses decides to turn aside to see this great sight. At the same time, the initiative remains with God. The presence of God calls out to Moses. The writer depicts the presence of God through several devices. The first is the angel of the LORD. (The term translated "angel" means "messenger" as well.) The second device, the flame, represents a traditional symbol of the presence of God not only in Hebrew religion, but in other ancient Near Eastern religions as well. The eternal flame, the device of the consumable not being consumed, gives witness to the ongoing nature of the presence of God.

The God Moses encounters represents an instrument of continuity. This is the God of the ancestors, a crucial theme in Israelite religion. The God Moses encounters represents a center for compassion. God sees. God hears the laments over the poor. God knows the reason for their oppression. More than that, God takes action. God comes down to deliver them (Exod. 3:7).

The continuity, compassion, and decisive nature of God represent central elements in the interpretation of scripture in the black church. Any interpretation that fails to give witness to the compassionate, caring nature of God, fails in the black church.

However, in the Exodus tradition, the presence and understanding of the nature of God never become vehicles for the manipulation of God. Moses asks for the name of the God that he speaks for to the Hebrews. God responds "I am who I am." (Ex. 3:14). The nature of God continually breaks apart the limits of any system.

The religious experience carried with it commissioning (Ex. 3:10-12). The commission was to a particular task. At the same time the commissioning meant that Moses gave his prime loyalty to God. Moses jumped into the middle of the contest between God and Pharaoh.

As Israel Stood by the Water Side . . .The ability of God to make a way out of no way shows forth again. God remains powerful, and the people of God, those oppressed by Egypt, accept that power. The Hebrews remain resilient despite the oppression of the Egyptians as a result of their connection to God. Nonetheless, the people of God remain loyal to the Egyptians as well.

The Exodus tradition examines certain polarities. The Hebrews' loyalty to God is contrasted to their loyalty to Pharaoh. The power of God is contrasted to the impotence of Pharaoh. The compassion of God is contrasted with the hardheartedness of Pharaoh. The Exodus tradition explores these polarities through the story of the contest between God and Pharaoh. This, also, is a contest between the marginalized, the people of God, and the structure of the house of bondage.

The structures of racism generate unfair and oppressive public policies as well as bad theology. Black people react to the salvation and redemption by God with praise and thanksgiving. The celebration of the civic values of the American Revolution consistently happens in the black community. It is a celebration of eschatological hope for the fulfillment of the civic values of justice and freedom.

The black church retells the story of the Exodus tradition. Black midrash in the Exodus tradition goes back to the very origins of the slave church as well as to the independent black churches such as the African

Methodist Episcopal Church. The best way to present how the black church has worked with this material is to share the midrashic method informed by contemporary biblical scholarship.

The contest between God and Pharaoh escalates with the plague stories. Ten plagues accent the power of God, contrasted against the feebleness of Pharaoh. The first was the plague of blood (Exod. 7:8-24). The plague of frogs followed (7:25-8:15). Gnats and flies are the third and fourth plagues (8:16-32). The fifth and sixth plagues inflicted the cattle with disease and the people with boils (9:1-12). The seventh plague was hail and thunderstorms (13-35). Every farmer and shepherd in the ancient Near East dreaded locusts, the eighth plague (10:1-20). Darkness covered the land as the ninth plague (10:21-29). The final plague was the most frightening of all, the death of the first-born child of every Egyptian family (11:1-10).

The refrain, "Let my people go," (Exod. 7:16; 8:1, 20b; 9:1, 13b; 10:3b) frames the narrative. God forces the symbol of oppression, Pharaoh, to recant and release the slaves, to let them go. The hardening of Pharaoh's heart results in further opportunities to demonstrate God's power and points to the irony that the "divine" man of the Egyptians presents no real opponent for the God of the Hebrews. In fact, the God of the Hebrews has to hold up the god of the Egyptians, or he would have capitulated from the beginning. But when God stops hardening the heart of Pharaoh, he has to let the people of God go.

The final plague introduces the Passover tradition (Exod. 11:1-13:16). God struck down the first-born of *all Egyptians,* from the child of the pharaoh to the child of the lowest Egyptian servant.[9] The plagues attacked all economic structures of the Egyptian agrarian economy.

God attacks not only the Egyptian economy but the Egyptian posterity as well.

The Passover material leads into the last of the miracles, the crossing of the sea of reeds (Exod. 14). The Passover story and the crossing story complement one another. The Passover story describes the ritual piety that empowers the act of liberation and radicalism.

The Passover and the crossing stories introduce the wilderness wandering stories in Exod. 16–Num. 33. The subtheme here parallels that of the plague narratives. In the former, the Pharaoh had to let the people of God go. In this material, the people of God must let Pharaoh go. These passages represent not only a symbol of liberation but also a challenge to the black church. The power of this text, for the black church, resides in the way that it outlines typicalities of black experience.

The black community has always been faced with the danger that it might internalize the message of a racist culture. Black self-pride must first destroy black self-hate perpetuated by a racist system. Roberta Flack, in her interpretation of the Exodus tradition, "Go Up Moses," says:

> Black people let pharaoh go
> Without you there is no pharaoh[10]

One should not make light of the difficulty of "letting Pharaoh go."[11] Pharaoh pursued the Hebrew children even after giving them permission to leave. Once again, the heart of Pharaoh is hardened by God. Even on the eve of freedom, God presents the church with a picture of a God that is more than an unambiguous defender of freedom (Exod. 14:4-9). However, this once again needs to be seen as a witness to the power of God. Nonetheless, this presents a problem in black preaching. How do we present the fact that the suffering we face is little more than an opportunity to give glory to God?

This picture of Pharaoh pursuing the Hebrews even into the sea rings true with black experience. The oppressor does not give up easily or quietly retreat into a more just system. The oppressor keeps coming even after he or she has ostensibly given up.

The persistence of Pharaoh struck fear into the hearts of the Hebrews. Pharaoh is a precursor to the slavemasters in the United States. We can imagine the response of those runaway slaves with Sojourner Truth and Harriet Tubman, frightened by the persistence of the blood-hounds and the trackers on their trail.

We can picture these runaway slaves crying out. They might have cried out as the Hebrew children did:

> Is it because there are no graves in Egypt that you have taken us away to die in the wilderness? What have you done to us in bringing us out of Egypt? Is it not what we said to you in Egypt, "Let us alone and let us serve the Egyptians?" For it would have been better for us to serve the Egyptians than to die in the wilderness. (Exod. 14:11-12)

The slaves, black and Hebrew, have at that moment internalized the perspective of Pharaoh.

In every age there have been blacks, in the church and outside, who have chided the black preacher to give up in the face of "Pharaoh's persistence in evil." For the black community, this amounts to an abandonment of the agenda of justice and those who maintain strict adherence to such an agenda. No black pastor can avoid the confrontation with the internalized "pharaoh" that is part of the black community.

Black preachers have, nonetheless, followed the model of Moses and repeat Moses' words, "Fear not, stand firm, and see the salvation of the LORD, which God will work for you today." (Exod. 14:13) The issue is whether the community will internalize the will and perspective of

"Pharaoh" or whether we will internalize the will and perspective of the God of freedom, who has set us free.

On the horizon we see the Egyptians; yet, in the midst of the people, the God of freedom works: "The LORD will fight for you." (Exod. 14:14a) The tradition depicts the God of freedom as a divine warrior. This theme occurs again in Exod. 15. God acts, and the community has only to be still (Exod. 14:14b).[12] Justice springs from Yahweh, the God of justice. Therefore, the community can let Pharaoh go. Here we see the goal of the hardening of Pharaoh's heart: Pharaoh and his troops move forward into their own destruction because of their hard hearts! God gets glory over them through miracle and ritual (Exod. 14:16a).

God does this with the use of a divine general (Exod. 14:19a). The pillar of cloud represents the presence of God. The intersection of the presence of God and the power of God constitute the keystone of the Exodus tradition. The miracle at the reed sea (Exod. 14:21-29) has its power not in the ability to contravene natural laws of physics, but in the ability of the miracle to be a sign. The sign makes clear to whom one should be loyal: "Thus the LORD saved Israel that day from the hand of the Egyptians; and Israel saw the Egyptians dead upon the seashore. And Israel saw the great work which the LORD did against the Egyptians, and the people feared the LORD; and they believed in the LORD and in God's servant Moses." (Exod. 14:30-31).

Black patriotism has first loyalty to the God of freedom. Where the ideals of the United States follow the theology of the God of freedom, such as in documents like the Bill of Rights and the Declaration of Independence, blacks experience a natural affiliation with the United States. However, loyalty to the ideals of the Declaration of Independence should not be interpreted as a willingness to follow Pharaoh merely because he can cite the passages in a document which his actions demonstrate he trivializes. Hence the *paradox of black patriotism.* Black people must be loyal to the ideals of a nation without being loyal to the structures of racism that have driven that nation. The black community can let Pharaoh go.

In every age the black church is tempted to hold fast to Pharaoh. The stories of the wilderness wanderings represent how this is outlined in the Exodus tradition.[13] The question in Exod. 14, "Why have you . . . ?" represents a common theme in these stories.[14] The community attacks the prophet Moses as well as the God he serves. The way to justice and economic freedom remains rocky and full of hardship, prompting the people of God to complain. What we hear in this complaint is the voice of Pharaoh internalized in the Hebrew slaves.

AND LET US ALL IN CHRIST BE FREE . . .The loyalty to process characterizes the black church experience. The church, through the Exodus tradition, challenges the black believer to go with Moses before the throne of Pharaoh to demand that he let God's people go. At the same time, every black believer is challenged to let go the "internal pharaoh" in each of us go. The black church has always been aware that this is merely part of the process which is not complete until black patriotism gives witness to the loyalty to God through Christ. As the spiritual "Go Down, Moses" points out, the Exodus tradition has a christological interpretation in the black church.

This christological interpretation changes the perception of the black church as well. There are two poles. Moses represents the first pole. Moses is the servant of God. The preacher in the black church should be a new Moses. However, this new Moses is informed not only by the old Moses, the servant of God, but also by Christ, the child of God.

The other people in the Exodus tradition are symbolized by the pharaoh. Other texts use the image of Satan. Pharaoh and Satan constitute political realities as well as spiritual ones. We see them as behaviors and attitudes that do not advance the race. Satan moves contrary to the God of freedom.

Black patriotism begins with a loyalty to Christ. The Christ-connection to the God of freedom demands a commitment to justice and freedom. Like the Moses of the Exodus tradition, we must go to Pharaoh or stand in the face of Satan and shout, "Let my people go!" Like Moses, the believers in the black church must constantly challenge one another to "Let Pharaoh go!" Black patriotism has a loyalty to the process of economic justice as manifested in the model worker, Joseph, but never at the expense of loyalty to Christ, who means freedom.

The God we meet in Exod. 3 we encounter again on the cross. The Christ is beyond categories. The social and political conventions of politicians and biblical scholars miss the mark when they are interpreted as having categories that substantially give us a picture of the Christ.

Christ represents the responsive elements of the divine. Preaching in the black church is likely to begin with how the events of suffering move Jesus. In fact, Jesus' ministry functions in the black church as a witness to the responsive compassionate nature of the Christ. Christ represents the relational, as well as the responsive, aspect of the divine. Jesus is in the family. The presence of Jesus, assured in the end of Matthew's Gospel, parallels the consistent presence of God in the Exodus tradition.

The role of Jesus as a point of continuity from the slave church to the present is well attested and most aptly demonstrated by the nature of black ecumenism. The one thing that holds black churches together, whether they are African Methodist Episcopal, National Baptist, Presbyterian, or any other denomination is that *Jesus* acts as a point of contact with the past and with each other, based on that contact in the common past.

Application: Sermon

Here we have a Thanksgiving sermon. It could be any patriotic sermon in a black church because the themes remain the same. The foundation perspective colors the rendering of the text in a most helpful fashion. Preaching and worship in black church tradition begin with the common past of Hebrew slaves, early Christian poor people and black slaves.

This sermon was first preached in an AME church in Georgia. The title was "An AME Thanksgiving." Here we have an example of midrash. There is a focus on the social meaning of the key words. The political power of the words interest the preacher and the congregation as well. For these words interpret the slave experience of slave women and men and their children.

The insidious nature of Pharaoh continually nagged the Hebrews. They could easily give way to the pharaoh in themselves. Likewise, the black community incessantly faces temptation to argue with God that life with Pharaoh was better than life in the pursuit of freedom. Rituals and worship enable the black church to stand in the face of this temptation.

The role of ritual and worship is to call the believer to a decision and to undergird that decision time and again. Decision is a key element in black church experience. The spiritual "Changed My Name" carries the line, "I told Jesus it would be alright if he changed my name"; this is a witness of the decision-making tradition in black church tradition. This was a political, material, and cultural

73

decision. Biblical narrative illustrates the call to decision in black church tradition.

Black church tradition lifts up two biblical models for these types of decisions: *the crisis at the reed sea and the crisis at the foot of the cross.* Who can forget the song "Were You There?" in this regard? The song points to the decisive power of such a witness experience.

The black church is grounded in both Testaments. The story of the Hebrews is perceived to be a forerunner of black experience of the community. The individual black experience finds focus through the examination of the life of Jesus. Even though the texts for this sermon are from Hebrew scriptures, the christological elements remain. SERMON The foundation of the Hexateuch, Genesis through Joshua, focuses on three concepts for the black church: God's miraculous salvation for freedom, recollection, and decision. Each concept, working with the other, fashions the application of biblical investigation in the worship and preaching of the black church, and they help us to affirm our common past with the Hebrew slaves as well as with our slave ancestors.

The first concept is the miracle of *liberation.* An examination of Exod. 14 will illuminate this aspect of black church interpretation. The second concept is *recollection* which results in a liturgical and ritual decision. Here the small historical creed of Deut. 26:5-9 will be instructive. This is the cultural element of decision. The third concept is *decision.* The examination of Josh. 24 will make this point clearly. Here the decision is made in socio-economic and political terms.

The Exodus tradition is formative for the black church. It was conceived with a sense of kin with the Hebrew slaves. Now the black church battles not to return to the house of bondage. The message of liberation is simple: *God means for us to be free, whether we pursue freedom or not.*

The reed sea was a watershed for humanity. It was a time for decision against oppression. It captured the fear that accompanies the move toward liberation.

The message of Deut. 26:5-9 demonstrates the way this history can be used to illuminate black experience because it focuses on thanksgiving and the sense of recollection. This Thanksgiving has nothing to do with Plymouth Rock, pilgrims, turkey or even American Indians. It is, for poor folks and for the children of former slaves, a thanksgiving of the Bible, not of television or movies.

The concept of recollection shapes the use of the scripture in the black church. The term *memory* shapes the black church experience. The roots of black religion emerge from the blood and soil of black radicalism. These roots nurture the ongoing gospel of the black church. The Hebrew term *zacor*, ("memory") carries some of the same meaning and function as recollection in the black church.

"And you shall make response before the Lord your God." (v. 5) Recollection is connected to decisive action in scripture and black church tradition.

"A wandering Aramean was my father." (v. 5) The term *'obed*, translated "wandering," occurs many times in Hebrew scriptures. Seldom is it translated as "wandering," it usually meant "perishing." Black church tradition does not find it necessary to choose between these two translations; it connects "wandering" and "perished" as being two sides of the same coin.

African primal religions were grounded in a connection to the land. The blacks who were kidnapped and forced into slavery were by religious training imbued with a love of the earth. The separation from Africa was one of the early deaths of culture for the black slaves, so the experience of separation from the land was a type of death. Also, in the ancient world, to have no home was to lack the economic grounding to live. With no land to farm, death is just a bad pasture away.

The term *Aramean* is also important. The ancestor came from somewhere else. Hebrew scriptures repeatedly express that this is the land of the Hittites, Hivites, Amorites, and so on (Exod. 3:17). Just as the Hebrews were not originally from that region, Blacks in the United States are people born in a land that is not their mother land.

"He went down to Egypt". The land of Egypt represents for the black church an anomaly. It is part of mother Africa and a symbol of evil in scripture.

The biblical equation of Egypt with evil can be understood by a look at the archaeological remains. The temples and pyramids and the like draw tourists from around the world each day. However, they also indicate the root of injustice in the economies of ancient Egypt, Mesopotamia, and Israel. They also provide clues to understanding ancient Israel's concept of evil.

A professor once said that one can build almost anything if one is willing to pay the cost in human misery and suffering. The Egyptian architecture, with fine-dressed stones, gives an example. The royal building programs that built these tourist attractions extracted a high cost for the peasants of Egypt. Scholars consider Egypt to be the prime example of a redistribution economy. The Egyptians took what resources were available to the peasants and redistributed them among the royal court and priests. The laws against dressed stones in Hebrew scriptures have as their background this anti-Egypt mentality. Given the reality of racism, we must be aware of the source of the anti-Egyptian critique. The anti-Egypt speeches in Hebrew scriptures are rooted in an economic critique, not a racial one.

"And sojourned there." (v. 5.) The success of the people in Deuteronomy depends on the recollection of the period of slavery and displacement. The Hebrew *yager* means "to sojourn," not only in the sense of traveling, but also in terms of being a migrant worker. Once again, the points of contact with the text and within black experience are self-evident. The ancient Hebrews, like American blacks, had to recall experiences as migrant and slave laborers in order to resist the tyrannies of pharaohs and slavemasters.

"Few in number; and there he became a nation, great, mighty, and populous." Egypt was not only the place of evil, it was the center for evil. God's salvation takes place in the crucible of bondage, not the comfort of beauty. The construction of the story of the God of freedom in this way accents the theme of the power of God.

The plague narratives make clear the contest between Pharaoh and God. Pharaoh was the god of the Egyptians. No mealy-mouthed Egyptian god could stand before the LORD of Hosts. No person or institution, even if that person perceives himself to be a god, can stand in the inevitable flow of peace through justice. Likewise, Deut. 26 assumes the power of God.

"And the Egyptians treated us harshly, and afflicted us, and laid upon us hard bondage." Verse 6 in a riveting manner outlines the atrocities. The Jewish scholar of ancient Alexandria, Philo, wrote that the Egyptians needed the Hebrews as slaves because they were such a voluptuous people. The Egyptians had disproportionate power and wealth. Therefore, they needed workers to maintain their system.

Here, black church tradition would remind the congregation of the pristine picture of the ante-bellum South. Miss Scarlett's white dress is always spotless, but in order to maintain the plantation, somebody had to get dirty. When any one group says they will no longer do the dirty work, a standard of oppression comes into play. The result is that the Egyptians 'anah ("oppressed") the Hebrews. This kind of oppression is not dead. Like racism in the United States, apartheid in South Africa springs like a leopard on the gazelle of justice.

The depth of oppression is not limited to the physical. Oppression replaces the system of affirming values and self-hate is left in its place. The oppression of Egypt is systemic, touching every aspect of the slaves' lives.

The depth of oppression comes when what we say about ourselves mimics what Pharaoh says about us. When we think like Pharaoh, we have reached the depth of oppression. The leopard of oppression chews on the working limbs of black women and men, yet more tragic is the leopard of injustice which devours their minds.

This oppression is related to the phrase hard bondage ('abodah). Obviously this phrase refers to slavery. Slavery was an accepted part of the ancient world. The sin of the Egyptians was not slavery itself but that the innocent, those whose only fault is that they were not Egyptians, were forced to be slaves. This racism is closely allied to sexism; the woman as slave because she is not a man.

Verse 5b is central in the text and in black community life. There is the ever-present threat of revisionist history, in which historians try to rewrite the history of their countries and claim that their systems were not really so bad. Verse 6 must be seen with verse 5, for it reminds us of the horror of slavery, apartheid, and racism. Without the repeated reminder of how stony the road and how bitter the chastening rod, the miracle of salvation is not taken seriously enough.

"We cried out to the LORD the God of our ancestors, and the LORD heard our voice and saw our affliction, our toil, and our oppression" (v. 7). The Hebrew term for crying out, sa'aq, is pivotal in this passage and in the worship of the black church tradition, for it emphasizes the present historical context and witnesses to another more authoritative context. The words of the old spiritual; "I Been 'buked and I Been Scorned" make a deafening ring.

Our cries themselves have roots in tradition. The One we cry out to is the God of our ancestors. The roots of Christianity for American blacks lie in the American Christian experience. So, while we claim that this is the God of our ancestors, former slaves, it is more difficult to propose that the slaves were Christian before coming to the colonies. The role of African Christianity as the religious foundation for the black African slaves of early America remains yet to be fully determined.

The gospel of the black church is that the LORD heard our voice. But experience is full of screams that die in the night. The affirmation that God hears is central to the black woman, battered and neglected. The assurance that God hears is pivotal for the rejected and often unemployed black Vietnam veteran.

The good news does not end with the hearing; God's verse 6b speaks also of the vision of God: "and looked on our affliction, and our labor, and our oppression." God's eyes will not be averted, even in the face of the violence of apartheid, slavery, and racism. God saw the lynchings in Mississippi; God sees the torture of children in South African jails.

"And the LORD brought us out of Egypt with a mighty hand and an outstretched arm, with great terror, sign and wonders" (v. 8). Our God is not lazy. God is not a television watcher who sits passively as the world flashes by, doing nothing but hearing and seeing. Hearing and seeing (verse 7) are only the first steps of redemption. The second step is that God goes to work.

God provides the locus of liberation. The LORD alone takes credit for this redemption. Political strategies by themselves do not bring forth liberation. Black church tradition has been connected to capitalism. Black theologians continue to debate about the wisdom of this relationship. The point here is that socioeconomic strategy, whether Marxism or capitalism, must be carefully framed so that it remains clear that God, not social strategy, brings freedom.

Black church tradition requires any use of scripture to give witness to the power of God. Our treatment of this text can be no exception. The power of God has a consciousness-raising force as well. A key term here is mora' (awe, terror). The action of God is so powerful it inspires fear and reverence. At those times it is foolish to be unafraid.

God's signs and wonders are for informing the public. God acts for freedom. Those who seek to hold back God's mighty hand and outstretched arm must be ready to be crushed.

Black church tradition is aware that its justice language has a price. The structures of evil and oppression will seek the demise of the black church. When God triumphs in justice, changes will occur. Those from the mansion must take to the field. The order that allows some to rest and to receive a disproportionate amount of the world's wealth will learn that justice will alter their lifestyle.

"And God brought us into this place, and gave us this land, a land flowing with milk and honey." (v. 9) Notice the parallelism between verses 8 and 9. It is not there in the Hebrew text, but the Revised Standard Version makes a good theological point that the second step of the redemption process, namely, bringing the Hebrews out of the house of bondage, is not enough. It is meant to be connected to the second "brought"—namely, to this place and to this land.

The use of the pronoun makes a complete transfer for displaced people. Now they are placed here in this place and *this* land. The black church began as a collection of displaced people. Now the challenge of the black church is to carve out a place here and now as the descendants of slaves in the midst of the children of those who enslaved us.

God has not given us freedom so that we might submit to the new slavery of welfare or workfare. The land represents an economic symbol, not only a romantic one. It constitutes the vehicle to keep one able to feed one's family, providing a source of self-sufficiency and pride.

Joshua 24

The miracle of deliverance, the thanksgiving and recollection, do not constitute the whole of the preaching of the black church. Ultimately recollection and thanksgiving lead to decision. An examination of Josh. 24 will illuminate the issues of decision and covenant in black church tradition.

There are four sections in chapter 24: the preamble (vv. 1-2a), describes the setting of the text; a confession of faith (vv. 2b-13); the invitation (vv. 14-24); and finally the making of the new covenant (vv. 25-27). The confession of faith parallels, in large part, the small historical credo we have just examined; therefore, this discussion will focus on a small portion of the invitation. There are four parts to the invitation: the initial invitation (vv. 14-15); the response (vv. 16-18); Joshua's reply (vv. 19-23); and the people's final response (v. 24).

"Now therefore fear the LORD" (v. 14). The statement of faith requires action. Theology in the black church has always been theology in mission. It has always been practical in the streets and fields. So the movement in this passage from the statement of faith (vv. 2b-13) to the invitation to action is in keeping with black church tradition.

As the idea of the fear of the LORD emerges again, God's

action on behalf of the suffering community can be mobilized against them. Therefore, the fear of the LORD is a proper response to the power of God. Here the Hebrew for fear is 'ibdu (from the Hebrew word 'abad meaning "to serve" or "to worship"). The combination of the two meanings is clear in black church tradition—God has been there for the black church.

The service of God consists of sincerity and faithfulness, legally and politically. For the black community, sincerity and faithfulness find meaning in the economic world of everyday life. Ultimately, it is a matter of integrity and constancy. The church has the choice between the God of freedom or the gods served beyond the river, such as Pharaoh. The black community, in the face of patriotism, constantly decides matters of loyalty and justice.

"Then the people answered." (v. 16) The people respond with affirmation. The words, "far be it from us." accent the community's way of distancing itself from apostasy. Verse 16 has the community respond that they would not abandon God in order to serve and to worship other gods. To abandon God would stand in stark contrast to the loyalty God has shown the Hebrews. The loyalty to God from the community makes a bond through the salvation history (see verses 17-18). Loyalty and decision come together at this point.

The "cloud of witnesses"—Sojourner Truth, Richard Allen, and others—demonstrate lives of loyalty to God. These stalwarts were loyal to the story of salvation, in particular the Christ event. This is the loyalty that prompted Sojourner Truth to work on the Underground Railroad. This loyalty prompted Richard Allen to begin the African Methodist Episcopal Church when he was refused Communion in a white Methodist church.

"But Joshua said . . ." (v. 19). Despite the affirmation of the congregation, Joshua gives them another chance to reconsider this most important decision. He reminds them of the basic incompatibility of the God of justice and the other religions they have known.

The decision should not be entered into lightly. The God of justice does not fit in well with other gods working for the structures of racism (vv. 19-24). Monotheism for the black church is as much a political statement as it is a matter of doctrine. There is no God but the one of freedom; any deviation from this is heresy. The decision to follow the God of freedom is a profound one. A person must consciously decide to let Pharaoh go.

The passage concludes with the people reaffirming their commitment to the God of freedom (v. 24). The result of this was a cutting or making of a covenant; it meant defining the community as a people of God, not just any god, but the God of freedom. The result of breaking this covenant would mean the end of the Hebrews as a people.

Likewise, the challenge of the slave church comments on today's black church. A covenant was made between God and Richard Allen, and Martin Luther King, Jr., and Sojourner Truth, and Harriet Tubman. The abandonment of that primary loyalty will result in the dissolution of the black community as a community.

Pharaoh and the rhinoceros represent the same basic reality: the internalization of the external structures of oppression. However, Pharaoh and the rhinoceros do not have to be there. We carry them around with us each day. Only through the Christ event is the rhinoceros tamed. Only through the power of the cross does Pharaoh get thrown into the sea.

Black radicalism lives in an environment of piety, religious rituals that cause recollection and decision. We are challenged to patriotism, informed by loyalty to the God of freedom and justice. We move in a tradition that blends radicalism with piety.

Chapter V

Suffering and Critical Awareness

The Foundation of a Quest for Witnesses

Through Christ, the black church can attain a unity not yet realized in theological and political terms. Such unity and partnership demand an interpretation of the slave experience. Creation and christology give witness to this unity in partnership; however, the absurdity of the slave experience in this context demands critique. We have already examined how black patriotism and loyalty interpret the slave experience. Now we shall see how the slave experience bestows the dubious honor of *critical awareness* on the black community.

Critical awareness is a different way to talk about what scholars call a *hermeneutic of suspicion*. Long before any black pastor heard the phrase, "hermeneutic of suspicion," black people used it. The theology of the master was preached by the white circuit riders to the slaves. Black narrative folk tradition demonstrates the absurdity these preachers put on the text in order to make it support the demonic institution of slavery. We then had to interpret what was happening to the biblical text as it was preached to us.

Preachers may be more sophisticated today, but the threat remains. Hence, critical awareness and the hermeneutics of suspicion remain characteristics of the use of the Bible in the black church.

Let me give an example from the Book of Deuteronomy to make my point. The text reads that if anyone comes and says they are a prophet, and what they saw comes true, you can believe that they are a prophet, unless they say, "Let us follow after other gods." Then we shall know they are not from God (Deut. 13:1-6). We can distinguish false prophets today as those who do not represent the tradition of unity, loyalty, and critical awareness.

The black community stands committed to the value of freedom espoused by the farmers of the constitution without accepting their racism. The patriotism of black people takes root in the interpretation of the Exodus tradition as a precursor to the experience of being black in America. The experience of slavery demands interpretation. The suffering of black people requires an explanation. The Bible gives the answer, but whose Bible?

Part I

What Is the Nature of the Black Canon? Black experience and suffering circumscribe the interpretation of scripture in the black church. The interpretation springs from a commitment to unity and loyalty. The critical awareness that black people do not deserve to suffer determines black biblical interpretation. Even the matter of the canon witnesses to this aspect of black church tradition. Black church tradition interprets the slave experience and black suffering by developing a critical awareness of the popular culture and its theology. Such critical awareness informs even an understanding of canon.

Henry Mitchell recounts a story of critical awareness in

his volume *Black Preaching*, about a white preacher who came to the plantation slave church to preach. The text of his sermon was from Philemon, Paul's treatise on slavery in the early church. At first a few people began to leave during the sermon; but as time progressed, more and more people left. By the end of the sermon, there was almost no one there. The white preacher asked the deacon why the people had not stayed. The deacon replied, "They knew what you were preaching was not from the Bible." Black church tradition marks a critical awareness. This awareness helps the black church discern the Christian experience from the civil religion of America.

Critical awareness confronts the way the dominant culture tries to blame the victim of racism or sexism. However, black church tradition does not end with the critical awareness of the limits of civil religion or popular theology. Critical awareness affirms that my world and experience lead in another direction, not that of popular theology.

Black literature, drama, and culture also wrestle with the issue of race pride. Critical awareness says, "Suffering is not my fault!" Race pride says, "Despite the reality of black suffering, I have a responsibility to the race!" The issues of critical awareness and race pride round out the core of black biblical hermeneutics. Once again, the combination of black radicalism and pietism come together. The religious experience of black people provides the pietist location of critical awareness. The religious experience of the black church provides a denial of popular culture and theology. Critical awareness comes from a religious reading of the black experience and renders a practical piety rooted in the struggle for justice.

Every chapter of this book has illuminated the fight against the internalization of the theological and political structures of evil and racism. Critical awareness enables the black community to see that behind the mask there lurks the rhinoceros or Pharaoh.

Race pride provides the cornerstone of black radicalism. When we internalize the gospel of freedom we find a new self image. Here radicalism binds itself inextricably to the Christ event. *Imitatio christi* and *christus victor* are not the facade of theology, but rather the core of black Christian radicalism.

We will explore the issue of critical awareness through an examination of the Book of Job. The ideas outlined above find interesting parallels in the Book of Job. We shall see in Job a practical piety that affirms the experience of those who suffer. Furthermore, we shall see in Job's friends the political theology that tries to blame the victim for racism, sexism and poverty.

Traditionally, Western culture has claimed that Job represents the righteous suffering individual. Nonetheless, some scholars have argued that Job represents more than an archetype for every person. Job represents a community of suffering believers. The scholars who point out the more relational reading of the book however, fail to note the politico-theological dimension of their claim. Only Gustavo Guttierez and J. Alfred Smith distinguishes themselves from this trend. We will proceed, like Smith and Guttierez, from the communal reading of the text.

CRITICAL READING: KEY ISSUES A critical reading of the Book of Job begins like the other critical readings, with an analysis of the historical and social context of the story. The next section outlines the structure of the Book of Job. Another section will explore the issues of literary types. The next section will examine the broad themes in the Book of Job. The final section will examine the text based on the broad themes.

Each section demonstrates that the Book of Job

outlines a political theology that promotes a critical awareness and critique of popular theology. The historical and social context were ripe for such a cause. The literary structure and types give witness to the nature of religious language of critical awareness. The broad themes become almost a systematic political theology for black suffering.

HISTORICAL AND SOCIAL CONTEXT   *Historical Context.* The nature of the Book of Job makes it very difficult to say when it was written and no references to historical events exist. Therefore, it is difficult to do more than guess about the date. Nonetheless, the theological similarity between the Book of Job and Isaiah 40–66 indicates a post-exilic date for the material. The suffering servant poems (Isa. 52:13–53:12), for instance, also portray the righteous as suffering.[1]

The language of the book also indicates a post-exilic date. The appearance of Aramaic terms, as well as words that have an Arabic-like quality, indicate a post-exilic date for the book of Job.

The location of the writing is crucial in order to learn the way in which the text is shaped by the life questions of the region. Usually biblical scholars name Palestine as the place of authorship. There is no reason to question this.

The theology and the language of Job indicate a post-exilic date for the material. Such a historical setting would make rhetorical sense. The post-exilic community struggled to interpret the exile much as the black community strives to interpret slavery and the black experience. The black community is the group of women and men who are the children of exiles; persons put into exile so that the machine of slavery might continue. After the Civil War we found ourselves free in a hostile environment. Likewise, the returnees in the post-exilic world found themselves in a hostile environment.

Social Context. Sometimes scholars talk about "wisdom movement." The term describes the community of scribes that lead education in antiquity. The term *movement* aptly describes the active quality of the people involved in the struggle with wisdom. The wisdom movement includes diversity and conflict, and focuses on teaching the future leaders of the country. The social function of wisdom literature has to do with nurturing religious and political leadership.

The wisdom movement exhibits a polarity. We see this when we examine the divergences of so-called wisdom literature. The first pole, conventional wisdom, finds a voice in the book of Proverbs. Conventional wisdom represents the common sense given the political realities. One can locate the origin of conventional wisdom in the clan (family) or the school. Both of these settings begin with human experience in the political world.

However, the books of Job and Ecclesiastes represent the second pole, skeptical wisdom. Here the theme of "mystery" comes to the fore.[2] The complexity of human experience outstrips common sense. There are limits to wisdom and especially conventional wisdom.

Each pole has a political theology that attends it. The political theology of conventional wisdom represents the status quo with a sense of charity. The skeptical wisdom raises questions about the institutional foundation of the political order. Hence the Book of Job as an example of skeptical wisdom represents a resource for critical awareness and a new political theology.

Overall Structure. The Book of Job includes an interlocking network of structures. Westermann correctly divides the book into seven parts. A prologue (chaps. 1–2), and an epilogue (42:7-17) frame the entire book. The lament of Job in chapter 3 represents a third part of the book. The fourth part of the book includes a series of three speeches by Job and his so-called friends (chapters 4-27).

A wisdom hymn (chap. 28) breaks into the structure as the fifth part of the book. The laments of Job (chaps. 29–31) provide the sixth part of the book. The seventh section is the appearance of God (theophany) (38-42:6).[3] Westermann excludes the Elihu section (chaps. 32-37) which is secondary.

A less detailed structure would include four parts: as prologue (1-2) and epilogue (42:7-17); a series of laments and dialogues (4-27; 29-37); a hymn of wisdom that interrupts the laments and dialogue (28); and finally the response of God (38:1–42:6). We will follow a simplified version of the structure, examining the Elihu section (32-37) along with the dialogues because they share genre as well as theological perspective. Similarly, the laments of Job (3; 29–31) will be examined in the same section.

The structure of the book telegraphs the theological agenda of this challenge to popular religion. The structure contrasts the separation of the poor from society to the reconciliation of the poor with God. Each section contributes to this message, as does the structure of the book as a whole.

Structure of the Prologue. The structure of the prologue (chaps. 1–2) signals key theological issues. The structure begins with a curse of the blameless. The reader is reminded of the blameless character of Job in verse 1. The contrasts of his blamelessness and suffering would have been obvious to the ancient audience. The curse signals the reader that Job's lament is specific. Here we find a prime example of a complaint.

Chapter 2 presents a second introduction to the book. The speech between God and Satan found in chap. 1:6-12 has a parallel in chap. 2:1-6. The themes of chap. 1 are further explored here. The structure of the third chapter is simple. The movement makes a set of relationships that accent the themes introduced in chap. 1 and 2. There are three sections in chap. 3. They are marked by the "why" on the part of the righteous sufferer. The first part is in vv. 2-10; and the second section in vv. 11-19. The final section begins in verse 20 and continues through the rest of the chapter.

Structure of the laments and dialogues. This section consists of two soliloquies by Job (3:29-31) and a dialogue between Job and his friends, Eliphaz, Bildad, and Zophar. Elihu's speeches follow (vv. 32-37).

The first soliloquy makes the point of suffering in human existence through the use of literary structure. Roland Murphy, suggests that the structure of chapter 3 accents the dichotomy of suffering in life. The writer, following an introduction (1-2), begins with parallel curses:[4] a curse of day (vv. 3-6) and of the night (vv. 7-10). The parallel structure continues in the "why" questions. The first question, why was Job born (3:11-12, 16), parallels the second question, why is life given (3:20-23). Another example of parallelism illuminates the movement from the general to the specific. The description of sheol (3:13-15, 17-19) represents the general affliction. Finally, the description of personal distress (3:24-26) outlines Job's specific complaint. The parallel between Job and those in Sheol brings us back to the theme of Job as cut off from the world around him. The structure begins to make the reader aware of the broader issues. Job's suffering represents human suffering. Once again, there is the movement from the general to the specific.

The structure of the dialogues and laments consists of three cycles and the Elihu speeches. Each friend has a series of speeches: three for Eliphaz (chaps. 4:1- 5:27; 15:1-35; 22:1-30); Bildad (chaps. 8:1-22; 18:1-21; 25:1-6); and two for Zophar (chaps. 11:1-21; 20:1-29;) Job responds to each of these speeches (chaps. 6:1-7:21; 9:1–10:22; 12:1–14:22; 16:1–17:16; 19:1-29; 21:1-34; 23:1–24:25; 26:1–27:23). Elihu's response (chaps. 32–37), following a different pattern, has an introduction and four speeches.

LITERARY TYPES   The *lament* represents a literary expression of justified or unjustified anguish. Two Hebrew words associated with the form help us get a better understanding of its nature. The first term is *sa'ag*, translated "to cry out." The second term, *qinah*, is a type of Hebrew meter containing three beats followed by two beats, 3 + 2. The result is a poetry that in terms of sounds limps along instead of the steady balance that one gets with other meters in Hebrew poetry such as 3 + 3. The lament is the crying out of a person(s) in a literary style which itself limps, or carries the mark of its anguish.

The *disputation* in Hebrew literature is a formal argument between two participants. Sometimes this is called a dialogue. However, such a designation fails to capture the emotional force and intensity.

Lament organizes salvation history according to the religion of Hebrew scriptures. The pattern of history, according to Israelite religion, was sin-natural consequences-lament-deliverance. This pattern is seen most clearly in the Book of Judges. However, it is also present in Exodus and throughout the Hebrew Bible.[5]

The lament organizes the Book of Job as well as salvation history. "If one were to remove *all* the laments from the speeches of Job, only the framework would remain."[6] The lament in Hebrew scriptures is the combination of personal and group pain.

Disputes in Hebrew scriptures have a long tradition and one which is theologically central, i.e. the disputation between Abraham and God concerning Sodom and Gomorrah (Gen. 18:16-33). The ability to debate with another person, or even with God, is a major tenet of the theology of Hebrew scripture.

Therefore, we should not be surprised that the writer of the Book of Job weaves the lament with the disputation.

The believing community is marked by lament, disputation and praise according to the theology of the Book of Job. As these three come together, no one element can be separated and still pay enough attention to life. The literary types give language to the political theology of skeptical wisdom. Lament and disputation come together, in critical awareness. When we encounter these together the result is drama. Scholars such as Marvin Pope argue that the Book of Job stands beyond any simple literary classification. On the other hand, Aage Bentzen and Claus Westermann notice the drama in the work. The Book of Job presents us with a story in lament. The political theology of the black church is a dramatic one that makes use of skeptical wisdom/critical awareness.

BROAD THEMES   The writer begins with the question of the nature of God and human suffering, by describing their limitations. The nature of God and human suffering connect to political structures. As these are transformed, the new themes that emerge are: (1) suffering and scandal in popular political theology, (2) structural poverty, (3) the believer as victim, and (4) the survivor of suffering as witness.

1. *Suffering and Scandal in Popular Political Theology*. The Book of Job is to the religion of ancient Israel what black experience is to the American dream. The American dream has become a nightmare in black communities across the country. The Book of Job questioned the theology of the Book of Proverbs, namely that good things happen to good people. Black experience denies the reality of the American dream—that anyone can grow up to be economically, personally, and spiritually a success. Inasmuch as the agenda of the Book of Job reflects issues at work in the interpretation of black experience, it makes a particularly appropriate choice for examination.

One way the people deal with the suffering of others is

by labeling them sinful, poor or both. Certain things become scandalous. A scandal offends the sensibilities of a group by violating its common wisdom; therefore, suffering is a scandal. The fear of the LORD prolongs (and some would say improves) life (Prov. 11:27). We hear this same idea today on Christian success shows. This places these persons who suffer on the margin or edge of a group, never in its center.

The scandal and suffering is like a seesaw. On the one side is a large, affluent, overweight white boy; on the other side is a thin, poor black girl. He teases her by keeping her in the air. He is in control. The scandal of the seesaw is that the little girl cannot come down on her own, and she suffers because in the air she can't achieve anything. Her suffering, being out of control of her destiny, becomes scandalous.

The issue of suffering provides a recurring theme in black religious experience. Black biblical interpretation reframes the issue of black suffering. It looks at the text much as a critical viewer might see the incident on the seesaw. The black biblical interpreter sees that in both cases there are structural realities that come into play.

The Book of Job begins with a certain understanding of the nature of God, a popular theology. If God is the author of our success, then God metes out our adversity. We suffer because of our sin, or so that we might be better individuals. No innocent person suffers, or at least suffers for long. Thus popular theology blames the victim.

When we see that the popular theology blames the victim, we realize that the theology is really a political theology which maintains that the present social order exists at God's behest. The poor are poor because of their own sin. Poverty, under this interpretation of God, cannot come from the economic system. Such popular political theology thrived not only in the United States, it was born in Europe. The term "popular" is used for two reasons: (1)

"popular is contrasted to rational or critical; it is taken for granted. As such, the popular political theology became conventional Christianity to the degree that it became the convention of the dominant political power; (2) The theology was popular with the ruling groups in whatever context. The colonizers resonated with the theology and attempted to have the colonized take it on as their own.

As the American colonies embraced the popular political theology, it became a cornerstone of colonial theology. The missionaries brought the "good news" of popular political theology to Latin America, Africa and the South Pacific. But not all of the colonial theology was to leave the United States. The slavemasters taught the same type of popular political theology. Similarly, in the period following the Civil War, the white church maintained that conventional Christianity provided the gospel for the freed slave. The preachers of the Word to black communities from Richard Allen, to Sojourner Truth to W.E.B. DuBois challenged this conventional or popular political theology.

Under the tyranny of conventional Christianity, suffering stands as a scandal. Believers do not suffer. When suffering and poverty ensnared a believer, such as Job, the result was a crisis. This crisis gave the believing community of antiquity the Book of Job. The writer rips apart the dead carcass of popular theology, and the message of Job is a poignant illustration of black biblical hermeneutic. It provides an opportunity to see a critical reading at work. The broad themes of the book outline a strategy for developing a new political theology to supplant the political theology of Proverbs, the most eloquent description of conventional theology. Proverbs created problems because it taught that only sinners suffer. However, life was not that way. The Book of Job gives us a model of a righteous person who suffers.

2. *Structural Poverty*. Our understanding of Job's

poverty can be translated into categories of structural poverty, a system much larger than the poor person but built on a society's need for "poor" persons. The poor are always with us because the poor remain an economic necessity in a sinful world. Structural poverty sets the poor person(s) apart; they are different, but not special. Job's friends and his response to them represent a dialogue on the issue of structural poverty (vv. 3-13; 14:1–21:21; 21:22–27:23; 32–37).

Let's go back to the seesaw incident for an illustration. If the white boy wants to continue to dominate the game, the black girl must remain thin. He has the weight, and thereby, the advantage. However, affluence gives him more chance to maintain his weight advantage. The structure gives him things and takes things away from her. It is a zero sum game.

3. *The Believer as Sufferer.* The suffering of Job does not present the problem. How can one believe and at the same time question conventional wisdom? In this case, the saying that those who suffer deserve to suffer presents a nagging question. The scandal is the way in which Job is both believer and sufferer. He calls into question the conventional wisdom about blaming the victim. These issues are addressed in the hymn to wisdom (chap. 28) and in the appearance of God, a theophany (38:1–42:6).

Christian and Jewish traditions have for years been able to understand the martyrs as believers who suffer. Now, the people who struggle in the grip of structural poverty and still believe, instruct us that there is a new believer as sufferer which tradition has ignored.

4. *Survivors As Witness Near and Far.* On Sunday mornings in pulpits all across the United States, black preachers ask the question, "Can I get a witness?" Who is a witness? The witness is one who has seen and heard and been transformed. The transformation not only enables

the person to be credible as a witness, but compels the person to testify. Like the prophet Jeremiah, for the witness there is a fire in the bones (Jer. 20:7-18).

The transformation brings with it a new awareness, a critical hermeneutic. The transformation generates a type of alienation from the dominant culture and creates the hermeneutics that undergird that culture. We have seen this in Martin Luther King, Jr., Elie Weisel, and Nelson Mandela. Black experience in America, the Holocaust, and apartheid so changed these men that every text, including the biblical text, has new meaning. Each of these men are survivors of suffering. Each of them is a witness as well.

The Jewish scholar Robert Gordis describes the Book of Job as seeing the contradiction between the group tradition about suffering and the personal experience of suffering.[7] He does not go far enough. Job becomes a witness. As such, the contradiction between what he has experienced and what he has heard of popular political theology can no longer stand. We shall see that those who would survive must witness.

Part II

Section I. Survivor as Witness. Job 1–3 introduces the motif of alienation. Here, also, the writer explores the idea of survivors as witnesses. The writer uses two devices to make this exploration. The discussion and description of Satan makes up the first rhetorical device. We see this in Satan's request of God that if the test is to be fair, Job must be isolated from God's protection (1:11). The description of Job's alienation from family and friends is the second rhetorical device 1:13-19) which recounts the loss of family and (2:9) which illustrates his estrangement from his wife.

The analogy of abuse describes the experience of

alienation, that is, the victim of abuse is separated from society as a victim. Further, the victim of abuse is asked to disassociate the feelings engendered by the experience. Job was set apart on the ash heap (2:8b). His friends asked him to ignore his experience of suffering. Likewise, the black community is separated through racism and then told by the dominant society not to feel rejected.

Who Is This Satan Character?

Often we think of Satan as the author of evil. Here Satan is depicted as the tempter. It is an English transliteration of the Hebrew term. [Transliteration is writing the letters from the Hebrew in their English equivalents.] The Hebrew means "adversary." Satan is the accuser in both Job and Zechariah (3:1-2). Satan is the prosecuting attorney in the divine council.

Earlier we found it necessary to name the serpent from the Garden of Eden experience and Pharaoh from the Egypt experience. Now we strive to identify the Satan in the Job experience.

The metaphor and reality of Satan, like that of the serpent and pharaoh, help us understand the power of popular political theology and how we internalize it. Satan sought to cross examine Job on the witness stand of suffering. Under such a cross examination Job was to defy the popular political theology and denounce God. However, the twist in the story line is that Job does, in fact, denounce popular political theology and refuses to denounce God. Satan made no provisions for the possible success of Job's friends. Job's friends so internalized the popular political theology that even in times of suffering they blamed the victim. In fact, they asked the victim to blame himself. The black community, like Job's friends, is tempted to ask the victims of abuse and structural poverty to blame themselves.

Survivors as Witness: Alienation

In Job 1–3 the language of estrangement marks the suffering. One of the early steps in the process of suffering is being set apart, quarantined. The phrase "and I escaped, only me, alone, in order to tell you" occurs four times in the space of five verses (1:15b, 16b, 17b, 19b).

The writer uses this phrase to bring the reader to a sense of alienation with three devices: (1) The term *melet*, meaning to "slip away, escape," underlines how uncertain the situation was for the speaker. The writer uses the first person, "I escaped," to drive home the theme of alienation, (2) The writer accents the words *raq ani*, "only I." (3) Finally, the writer tags immediately onto the term *lebdi*, "alone."

Part of the power of oppression in Nazi Germany, South Africa, and around the globe is the unpredictable way it strikes one country but not another. The randomness isolates in its own way. The survivors are allowed to escape in order to tell you, that is, us. Marginality contains the survivor mentality.

Job does not begin the story as a survivor or a witness. The story begins with Job as well connected to family and community. Suddenly, and without warning, adversity separates Job from his own family as well as those he cared about in the community.

The alienation of Job is a prerequisite of the plot as well as a characteristic of suffering. Satan asked whether Job would believe in God, even in the midst of alienation and marginality (Job 1:9-12). The test of faith, according to Satan, is how we live when we are cut off from our friends and even from our world. At times of separation, we come to the question of the nature of God with new eyes. If God is good, how can we suffer? If God is good, why "do I feel so all alone?"

Even in the midst of separation and alienation, the

connection between the believing sufferer and God remains. The black church resonates with Job as he says, "Naked I came out of the womb of my mother. Naked I return there. The LORD gives and the LORD takes. The name of the LORD is a blessing" (Job 1:21). The black church gives an adequate example of the ways the believing community refuses to allow suffering to cut the cords of affection.

At the same, time we need to look at the use of the term naked. Here the word indicates that we come into life at the mercy of our environment. For example, I was present at the birth of my sons. They came naked from the womb, vulnerable to the environment. So much so, that on one occasion we made sure that the lighting and the temperature of the delivery room would be comfortable for this naked new arrival. We are born and die in vulnerability.

Relationship amidst alienation constitutes a core factor for a critical awareness. Can the relationship live despite the suffering? Does the suffering we experience as black people have to end our relationship with God? Will we be able to recover our relationships with others despite the suffering?

What Is Abuse, Alienation, and Satan?

God places almost no limits on Satan. The Revised Standard Version translates Job 2:6, "And the LORD said to Satan, 'Behold, he is in your power; only spare his life.'" This translation is more direct than the Hebrew. Job is given into the hand of Satan. *Into the hand* is a metaphor meaning "in one's power." A limitation on Satan's power remains "his life/soul keep." The writer nuances both Satan's power and limitation in dealing with Job.

Abuse, Thy Name Is Satan

The text says that the life of Job was given into the hand of Satan. The term translated "life" in the Revised

Standard Version is *nephesh*, translated as "soul" in some places, meaning the life-force of a living creature.[8] The life force of a creature is that creature's reality. The soul is the vital part that gives expression to the world the creature senses. Satan constructs a situation so that the experience of Job is denied. The unjustified suffering he senses is denied by Satan, Job's wife, and friends.

Abuse is physical or psychological force meant to keep people from expressing that they see and feel a world different from ours. Abuse is a person's or group's attempt to deny the human experience of others. Racism organizes its own type of abuse. The experience of black people is systematically denigrated or denied altogether.

Loss of Family and Friends. Job loses his family in the series of catastrophes. He loses his wife's support in the midst of his suffering. Her advice follows that of Satan. Notice that the victim of abuse, in this case, Job, is asked if he wants to commit suicide (2:7). The wife is described as temptress, thus the parallel to the Satan figure.[9] The parallelism between Satan and Job's wife accents the theme of separation that was introduced in the previous chapter. Job is now cut off even from his spouse and partner.

Job's Friends Plus One

The process does not end with the wife. Job's friends then pick up the same idea. They send the message to Job: "What you feel can't be real." White culture denies the experience of black people every day. The lie of white racism denies the reality of black experience and suffering.

Another and related matter is the separation of Job from his connections. His friends do not recognize him (2:12). This lack of recognition accents Job's estrangement. The silence of Job's friends at the beginning also accents the separation between Job and his friends. We shall see later, however, that they may have been more together in silence than when they were talking. Nevertheless, the description of the friends' encounter with Job accents the lack of recognition and the lack of words. Now he loses his friends. They come to do grief counseling, and they stay, causing him more grief.

The descriptions of Job's suffering are painful for us. They hit so close to home. They remind us of those times when we were unable to recognize friends after a long illness. The text reminds us of the times we were not able to find words to express our sympathy for a friend. Such things are not evil. They point out the separation theme. Suffering separates us from our usual support systems. We see such separation clearly in the case of Job. Structural poverty and racism, today, create a community that is, a priori, separated from its support systems.

Job has a choice. He could disassociate (pretend that his perceptions do not exist nor do the feelings generated by those perceptions) from his experience of suffering in order to associate with his wife and friends. He could express his experience of undeserved suffering and thereby disassociate himself from his family and friends.

Section II. Structural Poverty and Popular Theology   The bulk of the book of Job consists of three cycles of speeches. Job has three friends, Eliphaz, Bildad, and Zophar. The cycle consists of a speech by a friend followed by a response by Job. We shall approach this material by looking at the speeches of each of Job's friends as a collection. As well as the appendix, the speeches of Elihu.

The speeches of Job's friends and his replies have some common motifs. The alienation of Job continues. The speeches never touch one another. Job and his friends never make contact. Also, the friends consistently assert that Job deserves to suffer. The more he stands for his innocence, the more guilty he must be. Undeserved suffering presents the friends with a theological impossibility. They assume God and politics are just. They don't want Job to question them.

I Can't Restrain Myself

Eliphaz is the first friend to speak. He, like the others, offers three speeches: 4:1–5:27; 15:1-35; and 22:1-30. The confession of Eliphaz leads off the speeches of the friends. "If one tries to speak to you, would you be weary, yet to restrain speech who is able?" The RSV translates this in a dynamic way: "If one ventures a word with you, will you be offended? Yet who can keep from speaking?"

This is the opening of the disputation section in the Book of Job. Disputation and lament are the style of talking about the human situation that the writer of this book depends on most.

You Can't Hurt

Eliphaz tries to convince Job that his reading of the world could not be true. It was not possible for a righteous person to suffer. A person can not be righteous before God (Job 4:17-18). The literal translation of Job 4:17 is, "Can a person be more righteous than his/her God?" The Hebrew word for "person" is geber. Hence the question is, "Can a geber, a strong person, be more pure than his/her maker?" The theological affirmation of this verse presents Job with a dilemma. He is caught between a rock and a hard place. Only the sinful deserve to suffer; however, everyone is sinful; so everyone suffers.

What is at stake for Elphaz is his understanding of the nature of God. If God is God, then the innocent cannot suffer. This doctrine of God becomes so central that Elphaz is willing to make sure that no one is innocent. He does this in order to save God. Eliphaz cannot accept a God who would allow innocent people to suffer. Eliphaz is not alone in his thinking.

Theologians and preachers grounded in popular political theology seek to find something in a black biblical hermeneutic that will protect their social and economic status. Theologians of this ilk might be reformers, but they can never be revolutionaries. The God whom they love has given a divine imperative to condone their wealth and status. Theologians and preachers of popular political theology have a precursor in Eliphaz.

Eliphaz then accuses Job of folly. He blames Job the victim. Trouble comes not from God. Trouble comes from humans as a result of their foolishness (5:1-7). Every theology has its own logical world and any theological position outside that world is deemed folly. Job's experience is folly according to Eliphaz's world of the popular political theology.

Eliphaz affirms that he has cast his lot with God. He explains this with an eloquent statement of God's action (5:8). First, God is the source of creation and mystery (5:9-10). Such a belief has a political side. If God created everything, then the political order, too, is ordained by God (5:11-16). God by definition protects the poor, so, if injustice has to shut its mouth (5:16b) then what we have must be just.

The popular political theology does make some allowances. The transition term, *hinneh*, (behold), introduces the proverb Eliphaz uses to make such allowances: "Happy is the person who God strikes." (5:17a) The use of this beatitude is jarring. Suffering is not only deserved but can be a way to being a better person. We find not only deserved suffering, but also instructional suffering. Abused children are spanked for "their own good," so that they might be properly instructed.

Black people remember the beatings slaves received at the hands of slavemasters. Beating was to inform the slaves of the existing limits so that they would not get killed by their slavemasters. Alex Haley in his historical novel, *Roots*, describes the "instructional beating." He recounts how Kunta Kinta [Toby] was beaten so that he would forsake his African name. Later, Toby was beaten so that he would not run away and be killed in the process.

Eliphaz's first speech has an "instructional suffering" theme. He says in essence, I have done the research. Your suffering is for your own good (5:27). The words "hear" and "know," found throughout Hebrew scriptures and especially in "wisdom literature," are connected to practical piety as well as the senses. These are doing terms.

Your Arms Too Short to Box With God

In his second speech, Eliphaz accuses Job of wasting his effort in arguing with God. He expresses frustration at Job's unwillingness to admit he deserves to suffer. Eliphaz and Job both experience frustration. Job does not listen to Eliphaz, and God does not listen to Job.

However, Job presents a theological problem. Marvin Pope in his commentary puts it well. "You [Job] even subvert religion." The Revised Standard Version reads, "You do away with the fear of God" (Job 15:4). Popular political theology argues that Job subverts religion. Any time innocent people suffer the political and theological status quo comes under scrutiny. Such scrutiny ultimately undermines the naive piety of popular political theology. Job subverts popular political theology and the naive religion it nurtures.

Eliphaz is trying to hold fast to his understanding of God. The core of his religion, literally, fear of God, is at stake. He then returns to the themes of his first speech. Now, however, his claim that humans are not righteous is expanded to include the heavenly beings (15:15). Once again Eliphaz claims that a human can not be in a legal position to argue with God. God is, by definition, above argument.

Eliphaz shifts tone in verse 17. Once again he tries to impart the wisdom of the wise men. The popular experience of the conventional wisdom denigrates any arguments with God by those who suffer (15:18). To question God now becomes grounds for sin itself. The person in pain deserves the hurt and cannot escape (15:30).

Verse 31 indicates that it comes to a matter of trust: trust in God, and popular political theology, then the pain will go away. The writer makes the contrast between belief in the popular political theology and trust in emptiness.

"Your Arms Too Short to Box With God" is the title of a play. It is also the theme of Eliphaz's speeches. God is beyond you. Disputation with God concerning suffering is useless. Such disputation is also blasphemous, as well.

Do You Know What Your Problem Is?

In Eliphaz's third and final speech he claims that Job deserves to suffer because he is too proud. Eliphaz sticks to his idea that everyone has done something wrong (22:2-9). The result is that Job suffers (22:10-11); God, on the other hand, is above this (22:12).

Eliphaz continues: Those who say nice things about God get good stuff (22:18). The righteous recognize that God has given them wealth. Here Eliphaz echoes Satan's question. Does Job believe for material gain? "Agree with God, and be at peace; thereby good will come to you." (22:21)

Those who contest God stand in sin. They demonstrate the sin of pride. Job's problem, according to Eliphaz, is his pride (22:29-30). The scandal of Job resurfaces here. Job claims that he suffers and it is not his fault. Such claims subvert the religion of Job's time.

Bildad

The second friend, Bildad, begins his first speech (8:1-22) with a note of impatience. He then asks about the nature of God. Can God pervert justice? Can the Mighty pervert righteousness? (8:3) For Bildad, the idea that God would not be just is so unthinkable as to be foolishness. If you question some religious ideas then you are labelled as heretic and foolish. Bildad, as a proponent of popular political theology, maintains that some ideas are above criticism; in particular, questions that question the justice of God or the social order.

Bildad's advice echoes that of Eliphaz. Job is to confess then he won't have to be poor anymore. Here, blaming the victim is clear. The victim remains the victim because of his/her failure to confess and repent. Bildad tells Job, "If you say you're sorry, God will bless you" (8:5-6). He goes on to support this position by referring to ancient wisdom (8:8-10). Job's experience contends that to confess is not the road to wealth.

Life in black America, like Job's life, demonstrates the foolishness of Bildad's position. The confession, according to Bildad, would have black Americans saying "We deserve what we get." The answer is, "I'm sorry" no matter what the question is. However, black self-blaming for racism has not put an end to racism in America. Confession does not put an end to structural poverty any more than it does to racism.

The text does not say that Job is creeping toward the behavior of the ungodly but the inference seems to be there. The rest of the chapter focuses on the fate of the ungodly (8:11-19). Even the end of the chapter contrasts the ungodly with the godly, who win socially as well as economically (8:20-22).

Bildad's second speech in Job 18 is short. The

impatience of Bildad is more pronounced (vv. 1-4). This ridicule is followed by a description that must have defied Job's experience of the world. The rest of the chapter maintains that the evil meet with disaster (vv. 5-29).

The third speech of Bildad is the shortest. It is a mere six verses (Job 25:1-6). The theme "Your arms are too short to box with God" is seen again. God possesses dominion and fear (Job 25:2a). Therefore, no person can be legally right in the face of this type of power (Job 25:4)

Zophar

A literary pattern emerges. Each cycle has the friends delivering shorter and shorter speeches. Zophar seems to only have two speeches (Job 11 and 20). The tone of impatience is clear here, as well (11:1-3). Zophar proposes that Job's language can not be allowed to stand; it not only offends but, also, places Zophar in danger.

Zophar then uses an interesting preaching tool. He makes his speech reflect what God would say if God spoke directly to Job. "For you 'My doctrine is pure, and I am clean in God's eyes.' But oh, that God would speak." (11:4-5) The passage (11:5) strikes the reader as funny because we know that God does in fact talk to Job face to face. However, rather than say, "Know then that God exacts of you less than your guilt deserves," (11:6b) as Zophar had expected, God's message is significantly different.

The next section (11:7-12) consists of a poem to the creative power of God. The creation language typical of wisdom literature is found here (11:7-12). The power of God parallels God's all knowing.

The turning point of the chapter is verse 13. Once again, Job gets the advice to repent. If you repent you get a long list of good things, outlined in verses 15-19. Zophar makes a promise on behalf of God. The promise is that purity brings security, lack of fear, confidence, and protection. But political realities witness to the falseness of Zophar's promise on behalf of God. The message of Zophar's second speech (20:1-29) continues the theme that the wicked do not prosper. The speech begins with anger not just impatience (20:1-3). Chapter 20 describes the fate of the wicked.

Elihu

Elihu's speeches (chaps. 32–37) consist of an introduction (32:1-5) and four speeches (32:6–33:33; 34:1-37; 35:1-16; 36:1–37:22). Unlike the other speeches, the Elihu series has one speech after another.

The shift in literary style indicates that the Elihu section comes from a different, probably later, time than the other speeches. The editor places the appendix at the end of the friends' speeches. We are not surprised that Elihu speaks last. He is youngest. Thus, the appendix does not jar the reader, on the one hand. On the other hand, the ancient near east culture valued age to such a degree that it was not the custom to have the young try to provide wisdom for the elders.

Following a short transition (32:1-5), Elihu's first speech begins with the strong self-image of Job, recounting his disappointment with the speeches of Job's friends. He sat quietly saying to himself, "Let days speak and many years teach wisdom." (32:7) However, he can restrain himself no more (32:17-22). As he puts it, "I must speak, that I may find relief; I must open my lips and answer" (32:20).

Elihu disputes Job's claim of innocence (33:9). Innocence stands as a metaphor for a good self-image. Job kept a good self-image for he had no reason for shame. He did not deserve to suffer. He could keep his self-respect. Job's contention of innocence meant a claim for a positive self-image even in spite of the experience of suffering. It appears that a positive self-image presented a problem for Job's friends. He was righteous, legally in the right, according to his view. They ceased to talk with him once it was clear that he refused to accept the position of deserved punishment as the root of his suffering.

Eliphaz continues the popular political theology. No person can claim innocence. Hence, a positive self-image by those who suffer or live in poverty constitutes heresy for the popular political theology of Elihu. Nonetheless, Job's friends now stood in silence. The assaults on Job's self-image were not effective. Job held to his position. He continued to say, "It's not my fault!"

Job's assertion of a positive self-image represented an attack on the doctrine of God of ancient Israel popular political theology, calling into question Israel's traditional religion that maintained that those who love God prosper.

The preliminary remarks of Elihu comprise an intricate pattern. Three *inclusios* make up the bulk of chapter 32. *Inclusio* is Latin for shutting off, confinement. In a biblical text, *inclusio* refers to the repetition of a word or phrase in a passage for the purpose of accenting a theme by setting it off from its context. The first occurrence marks the beginning of a passage and the second, the end. All that is in between is included or fenced in. Therefore the name *inclusio* is used to describe the literary way in which we are told what is to be included. The literary device is used to emphasize certain themes and indicates a high level of literary act.

We find the first *inclusio* in this speech in verses 7-10. The term *'amarti*, "I say," sets off this *inclusio*. The term *'amar* occurs over five thousand times in the Hebrew scriptures. Usually, it means merely "to say." However, here *'amar* has the force of confession. This is not everyday speech.

Elihu contrasts experiential knowledge and spiritual

111

knowledge. The latter brings understanding, *bain*. For experiential knowledge, he uses the Hebrew term *hokmah*, wisdom. It should be noted that this term occurs twenty-seven times in the Book of Job. Almost one third of those are in the speeches of Elihu (Job 32–37). He has provided a different model than Job's friends. The religious experience stands as another way to wisdom. It need not be tied to age. He now defines wisdom, *hokmah*, with the *bain*, understanding, of *mishpat*, justice.

We find the second *inclusio* in verses 11-16, set off by the Hebrew term *hochalti*, "I wait." This *inclusio* begins with a statement of patience, again (v. 11). Elihu scolds the elders for their silence. They have given up on Job. They have not been convinced by his critique of their religious stand, but they are willing to let God deal with the heretic. They have no energy to further the disputation (32:13).

We find the third and final *inclusio* (32:17-20) set off by the term, *'a'aneh*, "answer." We encounter the now familiar theme of the unrestrained need to answer Job's attack on popular political theology.

The end of chapter 32 provides a transition. Elihu claims impartiality. He says, "I will not show partiality to any person, or use flattery to any one. I do not know how to flatter . . ." (32:20-21a). The speaker claims impartiality in order to accent that the message comes truly from God. According to Elihu, the message does not conform to any partial political or social intentions. We know, nonetheless, that the time to be most suspicious is when someone claims impartiality.

Chapter 33 is now addressed particularly to Job. Eliphaz begins with a call to hear (v. 33:1). Then he establishes his right to speak (vv. 2-7), Then he quotes Job (vv. 9-11). These quotations have Job making two claims. The first claim of Job is that he is innocent. The second claim is that God is hostile.

Elihu's rebuttals are familiar to us by now. The first point is that God is greater than humans (v. 12b). He points to the folly of his arguing with God. He maintains that God does not answer. The Hebrew term here is once again r'ib, to be involved in a lawsuit. God will not show up in court, no matter what the subpoena.

He maintains that God instructs in two ways. God warns humans through dreams (vv. 25-18); God disciplines through pain as well (vv. 19-30). Once again, the suffering of persons does not indicate that the social order is in any way imperfect. The suffering is deserved. It also is a way in which persons can learn more about God's will for their lives.

In his *second speech, Elihu* addresses the wise (34:2), and calls them to make a decision (34:4). Then he quotes Job (34:5-6). Ridicule follows this call to decision (34:7-8). Then Elihu returns to quotation (34:9). Elihu, like Job's friends, argues once again that Job cannot, by definition, be righteous.

Part of Job's offense is that he maintains that his suffering is not transitory, or as we have said before, instructional. By denying that his suffering was preparation for some coming greatness, Job deprives the popular political theology of its limited flexibility. In upwardly mobile North America, poverty is a stigma only if one maintains that it is not going to go away. We see this in the way persons find the idea of structural poverty and a permanent underclass so threatening to the American dream. It appears that Job offended the Hebrew dream the way that the homeless scandalize Americans.

The denial of the instructional or transitory suffering presents major problems. As a young high school student I wrote a paper on structural poverty in America. I did not know the term structural poverty then, so I merely called it poverty in America. My English teacher thought it was a well-written paper. But it lacked insight. Nowhere in the paper did I address the fact that poverty is transitory. Abraham Lincoln overcame poverty. It was just a transition to greatness.

Further, Job offends Elihu by saying that there is no profit in piety. However, once again we are reminded of the beginning of the story. Satan maintained that Job loved God in order to profit.

One need only ask the people of the Pacific Islands and Africa if piety is profitable. The story is told how the missionaries came to their land. They said, "Let us pray." When the people of the land closed their eyes, they had the land and the missionaries had the Bibles. When they opened their eyes, they had the Bibles and the missionaries had the land. Piety provides no guarantee that one will escape a web of structural poverty.

The book of Job demonstrates how the religious order was connected to the political order in ancient Israel. God was just. The king, God's emissary, likewise, was just. God accorded wealth and power to the just. Elihu says with assurance, "God does not keep the wicked alive . . ." on the contrary rather God ". . . with kings upon the throne God sets the righteous forever . . ." (36:6-7). "Shall one who hates justice govern?" (34:17a).

One scholar titles the Job 34:13-15 as "Justice goes with world dominion."[10] This is a theme we have encountered before. The question of verse 17a ("Shall one who hates justice govern?") is so obvious that some scholars have maintained that the writer of this section must have been speaking tongue in cheek. Nonetheless, the reader must recognize that Elihu speaks from the sea of popular political theology. The statement is not tongue in cheek. The believer in the popular political theology perceives the justice of those who govern as an a priori.

When black people ask, "Shall one who hates justice govern?" the answer is, "All the time!" The speech would have us believe that no evil escapes God. However, for many people around the world, evil escapes everyday.

The third speech of Elihu, like the others, has quotations from Job's speech early on (35:2*b*-3). According to Elihu, Job asks, "How am I better off than if I had sinned?" (35:3b) Elihu says he will answer the questions of Job. However, Elihu does not answer, rather he gives witness to the transcendence of God (35:4-8). Furthermore, God does not listen to the empty ravings of a believer. There is nothing wrong with lament as long as one does not ask the forbidden question. Where is God, My Maker (35:10)? These laments God does not hear (35:13). Not only does God not listen, but it makes God angry (35:15). One can never complain about God in Elihu's world.

The fourth speech is the longest (chaps. 36–37). The speech begins with a claim of authority based in God (36:3). The theme is the same. God is powerful (36:5). God is not destructive (36:5*b*). However, the suffering that one experiences is an opportunity for repentance (36:8-12).

It is ironic that the theme of the inaccessibility of God would not be seen as a problem here, but rather the explanation. (36:26; 37:23). The transcendence of God is also the other side of the sense of the absence of God.

The three friends and Elihu have a few similarities. They seek to save their understanding of God, their understanding of power, wealth, and possession of the good life. This means the justification of their social and economic order. In order to get this done, they had to create an understanding of the human that blamed poverty on the poor. In order to save the political and religious order they blamed the victim. For it was, in their eyes, better to blame the victim than to box or argue with God.

The black community challenges the popular political theology. At that point, white preachers claim that we have misread the Bible. The attack on injustice in black experience results in an attack on the church that has wrapped itself in racism and sexism.

Section III. Hymn and Theophany: Another View Job's friends outline the popular political theology in the disputations section. The writer uses the hymn of wisdom (Job 28) and the appearance of God (Job 39-42) to outline an alternative to the popular political theology. These chapters explore the contours of the new political theology of suffering.

As in every theology, we find orthodoxy and heresy mixed together. The popular political theology of Job's friends illuminates the experience of the powerful. However, the experience of the poor and marginalized find no voice in a doctrinaire theodicy of popular political theology promoted by Job's friends. The challenge of Job means that the believing community no longer excludes the marginalized.

An examination of Job 28 and 39-42 reveals a political theology that springs from practical piety nurtured in a relationship with God.

A. The Limits of Wisdom

In stark contrast to the disputations, the theme of mystery takes front and center stage. Dialogue and disputation are not sufficient in the face of suffering. Job 28 breaks the literary flow of the book. The chapter interrupts the disputation literary type with a hymn of inaccessibility of wisdom.

However, the interruption is far from accidental. The placement of Job 28 figures into the book's overall structure. Chapter 28 represents the literary middle of the book; thus the writer draws attention to its message by placing the hymn in the middle of the book.

The structure of the chapter confirms the theme of relational and practical piety as the core of a critical awareness, and a new political theology. The chapter has three parts (28:1-11; 12-22; 23-27). The passage begins with a description of the human quest for gems (28:1-11). The images of mining underground are used here (28:3-5). Futility marks the quest.

The next structural element (28:12-22) begins with the question about the place of wisdom and understanding: "But where can wisdom be found?" (28:12) Humans do not know the answer to this question (28:13). Once again futility marks the search.

Verses 23 starts a new section. God's understanding and knowledge is contrasted to the unfulfilling probing of the human community (28:1-22). The writer connects this to the creation theme (28:25-27). God established and made the primal search. On the basis of this relationship of creation, God gave instructions to humanity, 'adam.

The writer describes human limitations with regard to wisdom in the beginnings of the first two sections. The writer contrasts that to God's power. Doctrinal piety, the search for wisdom, provides frustration as outlined in the first two sections. Now, the writer has prepared the reader for the solution in section three. Thus, the writer contrasts doctrinal wisdom and relational wisdom.

The writer accents this theme with rhetorical devices of repetition and interruption. Reading the text in Hebrew clearly reveals repetition. The Hebrew negative lô occurs in verses 13, 15, 16, 17, and 19. We have parallel negatives. Verse 13 makes clear that the human cannot understand lo yada. "It [understanding] cannot be gotten," according to the Revised Standard Version (28:15a). This is a rare Hebrew form of this word, sometimes translated "bestowed." It is a hophal, which is a causative passive, so most literally it would be "It cannot be caused to be given." Obviously, bestowed is better English. It [wisdom] cannot be "weighed." (28:16) "It cannot be assayed." (28:17) This is the process of

117

testing ore through the use of comparison. Verse 18 draws attention to itself because it breaks this pattern. It so surpasses that value of other gems that verse 19 repeats that it cannot be assayed or weighed. The rhetorical device of the negatives accent the futility of human striving for wisdom.

Thus far the writer has made it plain that wisdom is valuable. In fact, the value of wisdom exceeds that of wealth, namely gems. The writer uses repetition as well as parallelism to return to the theme of the inability to attain wisdom. Verse 21a, "It [wisdom] is hid from the eyes of the living," repeats with slight variation 13b, ". . . it [wisdom] is not found in the land of the living." Where is wisdom and understanding? The human community is groping in the darkness; wisdom and understanding are hidden from the eyes of all living creatures. Life itself, in some part, estranges one from wisdom and understanding.

The literary structure, the rhetorical devices of repetition and parallelism indicate the nature of the instruction. *Everything begins with the primary relationship with God. "Behold fear of the Lord* (Notice this is *Adonai,* not Yahweh. This is the only place this divine name is used in the entire book.) *that is wisdom, the avoidance from evil understanding"* (28:28).

Humans have the opportunity to be in a relationship with God. Piety also exists in a relationship and "fear of the Lord" provides the foundation of practical piety. There is a limit on human knowledge and reason which makes relational knowledge through God all the more important. The relationship with God shapes human action for human knowledge provides too narrow a foundation for action. Fear of the LORD characterizes a relationship of obedience, a practical piety.

While the search for divine wisdom is held as a good thing, there is, nonetheless, the awareness that decisions spring not from having all the information, but rather in being clear about the implication of the decision on the primary relation of the believing community and the one the community believes in.

No topic outweighs the importance of "my relationship to my God and my savior." When the time for difficult decisions comes, often we ask for more information, in hopes that, somehow, we will be able to massage the data, and that the evidence will decide for us. Our relationship informs decisions of practical piety, not data.

The creation language in verses 24-27 again points to the relational theme. We are part of the world and the world is part of us. We do not have divine wisdom, but a people of the covenant dare not avoid practical piety.

The vocabulary of the second part of verse 28 also accents the relational theme. The sur from evil is understanding. Sur means to turn aside, or a more colorful translation, "turn your back on." When we turn our back on one thing, we often turn to something else. No matter how one translates it, it is clear that this is practical piety. It is active.

The concept of the "fear of the Lord" offends many modern sensibilities. We think of the "fear of the Lord" as a collection of emotions and phobias. The "fear of the Lord" is at core a question of identity.

There was once a woman who worked in a large corporation. She worked her way up the corporate ladder and was given a parking space with her name on it. In this community a parking space was more valuable than a pay raise. She came into work one morning only to find that someone had parked in her space. The result was that she was late to work for there were no other places to park. She wrote a short note to the person who parked in her spot and put it on the windshield. It read: "I am Pat Smith. You are not!" The fear of the Lord in the Hebrew scriptures makes the point that God is God and we are not.

The fear of the Lord gives words to our awareness of the power dimension of our relationship with God. Once again, we find ourselves face to face with the challenge of radical monotheism. If God is powerful enough to deliver the Hebrew children, then God is powerful enough that the Egyptians should be mindful of the potential for their own destruction.

The challenge before the writer of the book of Job is to deny the deserved suffering idea while keeping the concept of the fear of the Lord. Traditionally, popular political theology has maintained that the fear of the LORD springs from a fear of suffering. The hymn of wisdom explores the idea that fear of the LORD involves awareness of limitations of understanding. The awareness of limitation provides increased incentive for a relationship with God. Human wisdom can never equal the relational wisdom of practical piety.

The believing community is in a difficult position. The Book of Job begins with Satan asking if Job loves God because of what God has done for him. Satan raises the question of belief for financial gain. In fact, Satan has uncovered the paradox of popular political theology. The believer does not believe for purposes of financial gain, but the believer does receive financial gain. Now, would we trade in belief for financial gain or psychological peace for belief based on fear? The message of Job indicates that if we are to hear the voices of the marginalized in our midst, we have to jettison the popular political theology.

B. The Visit from God

At the times we think we desire the absence of God. We long for the supposed freedom we would have if God did not exist. However, Job discovered the absence of God in the midst of suffering an added burden. Job asked to speak to God. He got his chance. Job received a visit from

God. The Hebrew term *peqad*, "visit," can be either a time of joy or misfortune. The visit or theophany, the appearance of God, represents a time of support or rebuke.

The theophany appears in three parts: two divine speeches from God (38:1-39:30; 40:1-41:34) and Job's ultimate response to God (42:1-6).

Three seams connect these parts of the visit: (a) Job 38:1-4; (b) Job 40:1-7; and (c) Job 42:1-6. An examination of the seams will suffice because traditional wisdom material surrounds them. The distinctive theological contribution will shine through.

Even the seams reflect the use of traditional wisdom literature literary devices and images. For instance, traditional wisdom literature uses the literary device of questions. Further, traditional wisdom literature depicts creation images as a way to point to themes of the power of God. Hence, the theophany (38-42) conforms in large part to what we would expect of wisdom material.

The seams in the theophany reveal the delicate balance which presents a God supporting the human community, but at the same time, depicts the human community lacking understanding of the mystery of suffering. Job is called to stand firm. Job is likewise called to remember who he is in the face of the God.

Before a detailed discussion of the seams, some general words about the passage might be helpful. This whole section (38:1-42:6) combines theophany and disputation speech. The disputation leaves us with questions. The German scholar, Westermann, notes that even the imperatives, commands, are themselves questions.

The theme of a responsive God also occurs in the laments Psalms (28:6ff; 85:8). However, often in the case of Psalms, God responds but also delivers (see Ps. 40:2-3). Here, all one has is the response of God. This theophany has elements of disputation and lament, but also is a hymn of praise. We recognize this because of the creation language that envelopes the whole passage. This confluence of literary forms tells us something theologically. Disputation for the believing community is also a master of praise. One can raise the question: Is there praise without lament and disputation?

The First Seam

The first seam explores this encounter and reshapes the identity of the believer, of you and me as believers, with Job. The writers pulls us along. We know God speaks to us as God speaks to Job.

God not only speaks, God "answers." The Hebrew term in Job 38:1 is *ya'na*, "answer." This term occurs over three hundred times in Hebrew scripture. Therefore, it often goes unnoticed by commentators. However, the appearance of the term in Job 38:1 accents the theme of God as responsive to the lament of the human community. The first seam indicates that our identity is reshaped by a responsive God.

The location of the divine speech reveals God's response to human suffering: it is out of the storm. Typically, we find the storm as the center of divine action and revelation in ancient Near Eastern religions. The use of such imagery demonstrates the continuity between the writer of the Book of Job and other writers in the ancient Near East. Some would accent the Mesopotamian connection at this point. Rather, I would argue differently: we see theological convergencies here. A number of religions recognize that God finds us not so often in the penthouse, as the outhouse. The location of the speech in the midst of the storm of human suffering conforms to ancient Near Eastern religions but, more importantly, it conforms to human, in this case black experience.

The Hebrew term *sa'arah*, "storm," conjures up a number of images. I remember as a child thinking of God as speaking in the midst of a rain storm, with thunder and water and wind. However, the image from the dustbowl years in Oklahoma and Kansas, which left many farmers destitute and homeless, provides a helpful context for reading the text. Another image may be taken from the drought of the southeast in 1986. Once again, farmers and ranchers stood on the brink of insolvency. In both images Job, like these farmers and ranchers, stands on the edge.

Job, as a suffering believer, is on the edge of society. He encounters the answer of God on the edge of life in the dustbowl of insolvency. In this context, the disputation begins with questions from God: "Who is this? This one who darkens counsel?" (38:2a) God describes Job as the one who speaks without knowledge. (38:2b) The writer harkens to themes of darkness and lack of knowledge earlier referred to in Job 28.

As noted earlier, the writer tries to strike a balance in the theophany: a balance of acknowledging the limits of human understanding, and depicting God as supporting the human community. Due to the writer's art, the balance comes through in every section of the passage. Likewise, we note the balance in the first seam (Job 38:1-4). The seam begins with the acknowledgement of the limits of human knowledge. Then the writer gives way to a statement of support: "Gird up your loins" (Job 38:3a).

We have all seen those who think it is funny when a person's pants or dress falls down, exposing their underwear. In the case of women in dresses, there is the threat of the wind that blows the dress up. The response of the person, who has had her dress go up or his pants come down, is shame. The attempt to cover themselves represents their attempt to cover their shame.

Shame differs from guilt. As noted family therapist and theologian John Bowman once said, "Guilt is, 'I made a mistake.' Shame is, 'I *am* a mistake.'" The phrase, "gird up your loins," means do not be ashamed, despite human limitations.

The term that is translated, "like a man," presents some problems. The phrase in English is tied to a sex role. Here the issue is status, not role. Status here means a place in God's universe. A role is what one should do.

The term *geber* is translated "man." However, the adjective form *gebur*, is translated as "strong man." The use of the term in Job 38 accents not sex role but strength. A dynamic translation might read differently. God challenges Job to "get in touch with the strength he has."

It is helpful to encourage persons to tap the strength they have as empowered people. Humans are empowered by the Creator. The theme of God empowering the suffering is seen here. On the other hand, it is not helpful to force a role on someone.

There is no place for shame for the believer who comes to God. God has responded. Now God will ask. Job will respond. The Book of Job allows us space to complain, lament to God. However, we must be open to what God has to say in this process. We are challenged to live with the limits of human life.

The Book of Job can be understood as defeat of shame. Job is not ashamed, but he is repentant. The result of shame is abuse and bad self-image. The result of repentance is new life. Repentance comes from the awareness that we have this treasure in earthen vessels, but we are not damaged goods.

Popular political theology seeks to shame and render powerless the poor in general and black people in particular. The critical awareness we find through reading the scriptures, especially the Book of Job, short circuits attempts of popular political theology to use shame to demoralize us.

The Second Seam

Chapter 40 is the mid-point of the theophany. Once again, God begins with a question. The RSV reads "Shall a faultfinder contend with the Almighty?" God calls Job a faultfinder. The Hebrew term *ya'kah* and *yasur* means to argue and judge. Job argues, *rob*. This form of the word is taken from the verb *rib* which has its origins in the legal setting.

Once again, we see the delicate balance of acknowledgment of human limitations and God's support for the human community. However, unlike the previous seam (38:1-4), which began with reproach and moved to support, (40:1-7) Job's apology interrupts reproach (40:2) and support (40:7). It (40:4-5) acknowledges his limitations. He makes the point that he is small. To press his point, he apologizes and says he will not repeat the offense.

After the apology, God encourages Job: "Gird up your loins like a man" (40:7a). The statement of affirmation here parallels Job 38:2. The human is clearly not on the same level as God. Again, the fear of the Lord, the metaphor for human acknowledgement of the transcendence of God emerges. However, the delicate balance offsets the rebuke (40:2). The human, in this case Job, is valued as human; his experience is valued even at those points it provides for theological conflict. There is a clear distinction between God and the friends of Job.

The language is, once again, one of relationship. The question and answer mode requires a relationship. The theophany affirms the basic relationship between Job and God. God does visit.

A further statement of encouragement occurs at the end of the sentence. "I will ask and you will answer" (40:7b). This is somewhat misleading. A more literal translation would be "I will ask and you will make known [to me]."

Again, the delicate balance of rebuke and support displays itself. This translation makes clear that the theme of knowledge is repeated here. In essence, what we know, limited as it may be, we are compelled to share as witnesses to human suffering.

The Third Seam

The third seam begin with Job's answer to God. His speech picks up on the theme of knowledge (42:2). In fact, knowledge starts with the recognition of God's power (42:2-3a).

Verse 3b begins with what is sometimes called a *result* clause. It is introduced by the term "therefore." A result clause indicates that the action following, the "therefore" is based on the action described immediately before the "therefore." Job's self depiction as one without knowledge lays the groundwork. Verse 3b following, builds on this framework and results from the assertions of Job's limited knowledge.

The limits of his wisdom comprise the heart of Job's defense. He spoke, but he did not understand or know. Once again, we are reminded of Job 28 where the limitation of human wisdom is offset by the relationship with God, described as the "fear of the LORD." Limitations and support go hand in hand; if the limits of human wisdom constitute Job's defense, the relationship with God, in the theophany, comprises the heart of Job's salvation, through practical piety.

The story does not end with the limits of human wisdom. Verse 4 returns the reader to the end of the other seams. The echo of divine questioning (40:7) is clear here. The term "answer," (42:1) as in chapter 40, comes from the word "to make known." This prepares the reader for the confession that follows (42:5-6).

The concept of knowledge is transformed. The confession is beautiful. The writer describes Job's understanding springing from the waters of experience. This is a spiritual experience. It is described in verse 5.

Beginning with another result clause indicated by the term, "therefore," verse 6 presents one of the central theological gordian knots of the entire book. The translation is unfortunate: "I despise myself and repent" is theologically unacceptable and linguistically unnecessary. Further, it contradicts the message of the Book of Job. Marvin Pope's translation is better. "I recant and repent."[11]

The recant and repent must be kept together. They signal the change in language, recanting. They also signal a change in behavior, repentance. The challenge before a people of covenant is to recant and repent. This will mean a new language of faith and new action in faith.

Part III.

Critical Awareness and Race Pride Not long after World War II, playwright Archibald MacLeish wrote the play *J.B.* The play explores the problems confronting people in an affluent society. The result is a very private and individualistic Job. Notice the contrast to the characters from contemporary black plays such as "A Soldier's Play," "Raisin in the Sun" and "Your Arms Too Short to Box with God." The Book of Job as dramatic literature provides a natural source for dramatic reflection on suffering amidst lament and disputation.

The book of Job warns us of popular political theology and, as such, develops in us a critical awareness. However, critical awareness is not enough! It provides a catalyst for race pride. By race pride, I mean the living out a particular political life based on the religious experience of the race. Black drama explores the theme of race pride and critical awareness. As such, black theater provides impetus for the conversation of race pride and critical awareness as dynamic forces in the community. The back drop of this conversation remains a critical awareness of black suffering.

In the book of Job the acute nature of suffering provided the impetus for the theological reflection. In black drama, the chronic and structural nature of suffering provides the context for theological reflection. In both, we see a search for an alternative to popular political theology.

In this section we will examine critical awareness and race pride in black drama as informed by the Job material. The first part of the section introduces you to the play and the main themes and images. The second part describes the characters Walters and Wilkie who seem to have most thoroughly internalized popular political theology. The third part explores the identity issues involved in critical awareness and race pride outlined in the play.

Introduction to the Play. The recovery of the theme of critical awareness and race pride finds expression in the Charles Fuller drama, "A Soldier's Play." Fuller presents a play in two acts, set in Fort Neal, Louisiana, in 1944. The black regiment, that has not seen action in the segregated armed forces, provides a key element in the social context of the play. The main characters are Tech. Sergeant Vernon C. Waters, Private James Wilkie (formerly a sergeant until found drunk on duty by Waters and demoted), Private First Class Melvin Peterson, Private C. J. Memphis and Captain Richard Davenport.

The plot revolves around Davenport's investigation into the murder of Waters. Each character represents a position in terms of the issue of race pride and critical awareness. The play provides an interesting juxtaposition to the Job material. Job loses everything and, in the context of conversations with others, explores meaning in suffering. In the play, each is a Job figure by virtue of his suffering. The issue for the characters in Fuller's play is how will they respond to the popular political theology.

Will they internalize it? What will they do if they decide not to internalize it?

Fuller describes the opening scene. Two points about the set are noteworthy. First, we notice its organization. "The entire set resembles a courtroom." Suffering and justice come together in ways that make the courtroom setting an appropriate device. "A Soldier's Play," like the book of Job, is acted out on a stage resembling a courtroom. Black experience and suffering provide the courtroom context from Watts to Roxbury, to Harlem, and what used to be the Fillmore district.[12]

The second aspect of the set illuminates the role of religion and role models in black tradition. In the background, the poster of soldier Joe Louis stands silently. The words put into Private Louis' mouth are, "We're going to do our part—and we'll win because God is on our side." The play begins with the juxtaposition of theological loyalty and patriotism. Further, one ponders over the comment, "God is on our side." Who is the "our"? Does one take this comment on the most superfluous level and say that us means the people of the United States, or does one propose that in the context of the play this message is tongue in cheek with "our" referring to black Americans?

The characters in the Book of Job also struggle with the issue of suffering and God's stand. Job's friends argue that God is on their side. Job disputes this. Fuller has the audience wrestle with the idea of which side is "our side."

Issues of "our side" also speak to matters of "our place." When Davenport describes himself he describes the black church in America. "I'm a lawyer the segregated Armed Services couldn't find a place for." Every character in that play stands without a place. Race pride strives to make a place for folk who structurally have no place. Critical awareness and race pride establish a place for black people and the black church in a system that structurally provides no place.

In "A Soldier's Play," the critical awareness reverberates throughout. The dying words of the drunk Tech Sergeant Vernon Waters, "They'll still hate you!" echo in the ears of the audience. Because black suffering does not begin with the black community, no penance by black folk can pay off the debt. They still hate you; when Job understands that there is nothing he can do to avoid suffering, he refutes popular political theology and the theodicy of injustice.

Critical awareness and race pride seek to refute popular political theology. They also provide a place for the black church and black people.

Walters and Wilkie. The Internalization of Popular Political Theology. The conversation of race pride uncovers the tenacity of popular political theology. Waters says, "That ain't no excuse, Wilkie. . . . Not havin' ain't no excuse for not gettin'." Waters has internalized the popular political theology. Waters' statement betrays his position and illustrates the temptation of black religion as popular political theology in blackface. Like Job's friends, Waters argues that black suffering is to some degree deserved, and on the other hand, transitory and instructive.

The exploration of the hope and aspirations for black youth consistently provides a background for the discussion of race pride. When Waters tells Wilkie about his hope for his son he makes this clear. "I couldn't do any better—and this army was the closest I figured the white man would let me get to any kind of authority. No, the army ain't for this boy." [Reference to Waters' son.]

However, Water's vision for his children is different from that of other black characters. Water sees education and being socialized in dominant culture as central for the advancement of the race. "I's sendin' bot' of 'em

[Waters' son and daughter] to some big white college—let 'em rub elbows with the whites, learn the white man's language—how he does things. Otherwise, we'll be left behind—you can see it in the army. White man runnin' rings around us."

This represents an issue for such things as how people think. Waters says to Wilkie, "Stop thinkin' like a niggah!" A "niggah" is anyone black who has not thoroughly internalized popular political theology, according to Waters. It seems that Wilkie has not internalized popular political theology as thoroughly as Waters, although he has, to some degree. We see the internalization in Waters' speeches of hope, but also in Wilkie's speech about the disappointment on the loss of his stripes. Wilkie says, "Y'all ain't neva' had nothin', that's why you can't understand a man like me!" Those who have internalized the popular political theology in the black community have lost their community. They have lost their own souls.

Critical Awareness, Race Pride and Social Identity. The center of the play revolves around the question, "What kinda colored man are you?" (p. 9) Peterson asks the question to Waters, but the black audience hears the question in their own ears as well. The context of suffering causes the question, "What kinda colored person are you?" to reverberate in our heads.

The play describes the double bind of these men. The white men in the oufit wanted the black baseball players to win for the regiment. The black baseball players consistently played against white teams. Consequently, losing and winning both posed a disastrous problem. "Every time we beat them (white folk) at baseball, they (white folk) get back at us every way they can." This is the context of the question: "What kinda colored man are you?"

The question "What kinda colored man are you?" lays

the foundation for critical awareness. Without critical awareness the pain of suffering takes on self-hate. Critical awareness and race pride give a necessary sense of place that avoids self-hate. C.J. Memphis, who serves as court jester, correctly notes, "Any man ain't sure where he belongs must be in a whole lotta pain." Waters had so internalized popular political theology that he no longer had a place.

Critical awareness and race pride demand that someone confront the model of self-hate. Sergeant Waters stands for the model of self-hate. Peterson notes "Somebody's got to fight him." The survivor of black suffering who has not internalized popular political theology must stand as witness against it. In this case, that means against Waters. The suffering that creates critical awareness and race pride can also breed tyranny. Just as the survivor of black suffering must witness against Waters, he must destroy, through tyranny, all those who do not conform to his popular political theology.

We find in Waters a tyranny born of hope. Waters, like many black Americans, thought that patriotism and heroism during World War I would demonstrate the fallacy of racism. However, "The First War, it didn't change much for us, boy—but this one—it's gonna change a lot of things." Waters blamed the lack of black progress on the inability, from his perspective, of blacks to internalize the gospel of popular political theology.

Waters never answers the question, "What kinda colored man are you?" However, Waters decides who represents the appropriate model of the new colored man. More to the point, he seeks to destroy all those who do not conform to his understanding of race pride.

Waters represents not only the character of Job's friends but ultimately, Pontus Pilate as he executes C. J. Memphis. For his self-hate now focuses on others, in this case, C. J. Memphis. Waters says to C. J., "The black race cannot afford you no more." Waters' vendetta on all those who deviate from his understanding is rooted in his hope. ". . . the only thing that can move the race is power." Waters' action becomes clear he must make sure that there is "one less fool for the race to be ashamed of!" C. J. correctly described the self-hate of Waters when C. J. compared him to a relentless dog. "So, you had to cheat that dog outta' bitin' you every time. Every time."

Peterson functions much like Job's friends. He asks the right questions but presses the wrong points. Peterson decides to protest Waters' behavior. Cobb says, "Peterson was right on that one-somebody needed to protest that man!" However, when Peterson's protest turns to murder, it sours. Now, the protest becomes "the Cain and Abel story of the week." Peterson killed Waters just as Job's friends killed him, through making light of his suffering.

Christological Reflection   Job, his friends, Waters, Peterson, and C. J. provide us with tragic figures. Some, such as Waters and Job's friends, are locked in the popular religion of their age. Even Peterson, who seems to be trying to break away, finds failure not redemption.

However, like Job, the black community has always affirmed "for I know that my redeemer lives, and at last my redeemer will stand upon the earth." (Job 19:25) Job and Waters both had hope. Job's critical awareness of the popular religion around him separates Job from Waters. The Redeemer becomes the vehicle for change. Job knows he can not save himself. Waters deludes himself into thinking he can.

The vision of the victorious Christ saves us from a race pride that fuels race tyranny. The witness of the victorious Christ means that we do not strive for the correct public policy that will bring our freedom. We are simply doers of the Word. We strive to be faithful to God who will, through Christ, bring our freedom. Critical awareness enables us to hear the words of Waters, "They'll still hate you," and not be struck powerless. We seek not the love of white folk, but rather, the love of the God of justice who sent us the Christ.

Through Christ, we have a model beyond Job and his friends, beyond Waters and the men of his troop. The imitation of Christ means living out an alternative to the popular political theology, a religion of the comfortable that makes light of the suffering of the poor.

The application of critical awareness and race pride pushes us to the question of a black political theology. Two component parts of this issue come out of the reflection on suffering and critical awareness and the context of the black community today. The first element is the stance of theodicy and ethics of the black church. The second element involves an economic program.

Theodicy and ethic in the black church. Here the watch word comes from our reflection on the Book of Job and black suffering. Critical awareness teaches us that our economic situation is not our fault. However, it remains our responsibility. Critical awareness demonstrates to us the structural issues of poverty. Moreover, if we internalize the message that our economic situation is our fault, paralysis occurs. When we internalize the fault we give witness to our powerlessness. When we focus on fault we sabotage structural change. The issues then become versions of individual character traits such as perseverance and industry.

Responsibility, on the other hand, provides newly-informed stewardship. Here we take our role as a power. Responsibility begins with response. We feel. The roots of a black political theology come from passion and compassion.

The second element of the term responsibility tells us something of power. Responsibility involves the ability to respond. We move beyond passion and compassion into structural change, seizing the power to carry out structural change.

If we look at the Book of Job, we see the movement from fault theology to a responsibility theology. The dialogues, as described above, recount the denial of the "fault" element in popular political theology. The theophany provides us with a picture of Job's conversion. Job leaves the popular political theology of "fault" which no longer has meaning for his experience and his status as a marginal person. Job repents and becomes a responsible steward.

If we review the lessons of "A Soldier's Play" we find that responsibility must be rightly apprehended. The Job story ends before we know the particulars of Job's life in this new stewardship. The play begins with the question of responsibility and race pride.

The play describes three alternatives. Two of the alternatives represent misapprehensions of responsibility. The murdered Sergeant Waters failed to recognize his responsibility to the very end. In his words "They'll still hate you" he hangs on to the "It's my fault. I can change my life only by becoming white." However, in his drunken stupor he recognizes the absurdity of such a position for "They'll still hate you."

The second alternative provides an unsatisfactory solution. Waters had internalized popular political theology. Somebody had to stop Waters. Murder, however, provided no arresting power for the struggle Waters presented. Waters and his murderer both face the recrimination of the black community.

The play refuses to fully articulate the third alternative. Instead, the play closes with the affirmation that on the horizon we find change for the black community. The playwright, with deft skill, challenges the audience to articulate the third alternative in their lives.

The first and third alternatives put forth an economic

plan. Now we will examine what such a plan might look like in our present economic context. Three elements provide the legs for a viable economic program: full employment, full education, and maximum decentralization.

Full Employment. Scripture and the American dream both presuppose full employment. Every person who wants a job should be able to find work which involves sufficient remuneration so that they might be able to feed, clothe, and house themselves. Three goals must be achieved for blacks to find such a circumstance.

First, the trade and budget deficit must be addressed. Until that takes place, people can make more money without providing good or services. Such a situation makes for fewer workers. At present, we find ourselves in a situation where the more billion-dollar merger deals go through, the fewer jobs there are for those who want to provide the goods and services.

Second, we must make sure that the increased jobs for blacks are jobs that make enough to provide for the basic necessities of life: food, housing, and health. Just as blacks are getting into the unions it seems the unions are losing strength. Black factory workers are either making less on the manufacturing line or are now working in service jobs, which pay less from the beginning. The number of black working poor increases daily.

Third, we must strive for a public policy that provides for a strong American industry. Neither the adversarial relationship with industry nor the social Darwinism of the market place will provide for the needs of black America. We must be at the table that forges a new American economic policy which is pro-industry, which includes being pro-worker.

Full Education. The black community has always viewed education as the avenue to success. The black college movement in this country bears witness to this fact. However, our reversals in education have been significant. The challenges to black education require money. We seek to provide education for tomorrow's technology. Also, we must continue to be the place where humanities that inform the life of black intelligentsia spring from.

Maximum Decentralization. Some politicians mistake deregulation for decentralization. The result is a world where the structural forces for greed outstrip the marginalized powers for responsible stewardship. A good environment for small business and farms provides a healthy place for black business people and farmers.

Critical awareness and race pride, as informed by scripture and black church tradition, challenge us to help forge American economic policy. The threat to black churches of the popular political theology is that it seduces us into abdicating our power. As God said to Job: "Gird up your loins!" Through critical awareness and race pride let us heed these words from God.

The political theology of the black church does not depend on the shaping of public policy. Rather, it depends on the keeping of the gospel. The political theology of the black church begins with the affirmation that our redeemer lives and shall ultimately be victorious. We imitate the Christ who preached that message in all that Jesus did. It is the witness of Christ, not the efficacy of the table of public policy, that beckons us.

The vision of speaking and doing the truth can be seen in the person of Rosa Parks. She preached one of the most eloquent sermons of black church history. She sat for the truth and did not stand for a lie. It was not a matter of public policy, but rather, a matter of public witness to the God of freedom.

The litmus test of preaching and application of black biblical hermeneutics remains the truth in the midst of the lie of racism. Black church tradition nurtures a critical awareness of the lie that black people are surrounded by everyday.

God gave birth to the black church in a time of trouble and travail. The crisis of racism strikes at the core of the black church. Popular theology does not work for black people. Popular theology understands suffering as an acute response to sin. The structural suffering engendered by racism has no place in popular theology. Whenever the popular theology, especially of the powerful, does not work for the marginalized, a crisis occurs.

Political theology of the United States, sometimes called civil religion, provides the popular theology of many Americans, black and white. Black political theology must eschew the focus on public policy that focuses popular theology as well as the liberal versions of political theology.

Chapter VI

Recovery of a Black Biblical Tradition

A Concluding Summary

For freedom Christ has set us free; stand fast therefore, and do not submit again to the yoke of slavery (Gal. 5:1, RSV). Together we have explored the black churches' attempt to stand fast for freedom.

Certain common threads appear time and again, for instance, the process of reading the Bible in the black church involves the mixture of black radicalism and piety. Other common threads involve an understanding of the threat to the black church, the method of reading the Bible in the black church, and the centrality of the Christ event in the life of black biblical reflection.

The threat to the black church comes from the popular political theology. We face the temptation to internalize this theology that permeates the dominant culture. Instead, reading the Bible in the black church provides an alternative to the popular political theology. The adversarial relationship between the black church as a believing community and the dominant culture is a recurring characteristic.

We noted a common exegetical style and method. The

method has three movements. The movements interact dynamically. The critical reading of the biblical text represents one such movement. The text must be read intrinsically, without the benefit of other books and resources. Another movement involves the recovery of black biblical tradition. Using an extrinsic reading of the text is helpful, informed by other books that help shape the meaning from the text. Yet another movement entails the application of the scripture in the life of the black community.

The critical reading provides the black church with a picture of the biblical text grounded in the political, social, and economic realities of antiquity. The movement of critical reading constitutes the re-apprehension of the text by the black community. Critical reading of scripture is part of black church tradition. The social circumstance of scripture parallels that of marginalized people the world over, including black people. The critical reading of the text renders to us a picture of the religion of scripture as ultimately the religion of the marginalized.

Scripture itself commends another movement to us, that of recovery of black biblical interpretation gives witness to the dynamic relationship between culture and religion. In scripture we note the interaction and sometime conflict between culture and piety. The black community plays out the same dynamic relationship. The interpretation of scripture and biblical themes occurs not only in poetry, spiritual fiction and drama, but also visual art, and music.

The themes demonstrated how black culture interacts with scripture to reconstrue the scripture as well as black culture. An examination of James Weldon Johnson's "The Creation" revealed how the black community managed issued of partnership and unity of life. We noted the break and the redemption of partnership in the fiction of Alice Walker. We investigated the spirituals for the theme of loyalty and partnership. Using Charles Fuller's "A Soldier's Play," black drama illuminated the theme of suffering and critical awareness.

Black church experience commends yet a third movement to us. Application of scripture dominates black church tradition. As black radicalism and black pietism come together, the matter of application becomes central. Such pragmatism has, at times, made black biblical theology appear anti-intellectual. The present study has stated the importance of application but has not developed the application sections in detail. Such an expansion would constitute a second volume. Nonetheless, any book of black biblical interpretation must come to grips with the application of the text in the life of the black church.

Another common thread was the importance of christological reflection. Christ breaks into the three movements as Christ breaks into all aspects of black church life. Before the application moment takes place the interpreter has to reflect on the christological implications. The black church demonstrates a tradition of apocalyptic Christianity. The christology of the black church responds to the apocalyptic roots of the church.

The motifs of the imitation of Christ always moves in tandem with the victorious Christ. However, as we explored we found that the victorious Christ provides the foundation for apocalyptic hope. The piety through the imitation of Christ connects with the radicalism of the victorious apocalyptic Christ.

The three movements provided structure for the examination of the black experience through three themes, unity, patriotism, and suffering/critical awareness. The themes organized the reading of sections of scripture, the examination of black culture, and types of black theology.

The themes gave us an opportunity to examine biblical narrative as well as poetry. We examined unity and partnership in the Genesis material. We looked at patriotism and loyalty in the material from Gen. 37–Josh. 24. We explored the themes of suffering and critical awareness in the book of Job.

The themes presented three types of black biblical theology. The theme of unity and partnership provides an avenue to survey issues in pastoral theology. The theme of patriotism and loyalty informs a liturgical theology of the black church. The theme of suffering and critical awareness provides us with the beginning of a new political theology.

Each chapter progresses in a slightly different fashion despite the common threads. The chapter on unity traces the belief in unity of life and faith in the black community. Piety and partnership provide us with helpful watchwords in this chapter. Here our conversation partners are the black literary traditions of poetry and short story. Once we established the reality of partnership, we explore the blocks to partnership. The exploration uncovers the role of black self-hate as a detriment to the black family.

The next chapter dealt with loyalty and patriotism. In this chapter, piety and partnership are replaced with the watchwords, piety and activism. Black spirituals gave us an opportunity to explore the style and content of black biblical midrash on the Exodus-Conquest traditions in scripture.

This chapter outlines the breakdown of loyalty, similar to the blocks to partnership in the previous chapter. During the critical reading of the text we discover parallels between the black experience and the narration of the Egyptian experience for the Hebrews. We noted the unrequited loyalty from the worker/slave to the employer taskmaster, one notable example being Joseph. We also noted the loyalty between marginalized people. The story of the Hebrew midwives made this point eloquently. Further, we recognized a link between loyalty and activism through resistance to oppressive systems.

The chapter on loyalty contained the longest application section of any of the chapters. Here we found a sermon text. The sermon gave voice to the emerging political theology we find as the black church reads the Bible.

> Finally, be strong in the Lord and in the strength of God's might. Put on the whole armor of God, that you might be able to stand against the wiles of the devil. For we are not contending with flesh and blood, but against principalities, against the powers, against the world rulers of this present darkness, against the spiritual hosts of wickedness in the heavenly places. Therefore put on the whole armor of God that you may be able to stand in the evil day. (Eph. 6:10-13a)

Notes

Notes to Chapter 1

1. Cain H. Felder, *Troubling Biblical Waters: Race, Class and Family* (New York: Orbis Books, 1990), p. 6.
2. Vincent Wimbush, "Biblical-Historical Study as Liberation: Toward an Afro-Christian Hermeneutic," *The Journal of Religious Thought*, vol. 42, no. 2 (Fall-Winter, 1984-1985):10.
3. Cornel West, *Prophesy Deliverance! An Afro-American Revolutionary Christianity* (Philadelphia: Westminster, 1982), p. 22.
4. W.E.B. DuBois, *The Souls of Black Folk* (New York: Fawcett, 1961). pp. 13-14.

Notes to Chapter 2

1. Michel Clevenot, *Materialist Approaches to the Bible* (Maryknoll: Orbis, 1985). The work of Clevenot serves as a helpful background. Also, my own work on materialistic approach to scripture and archeology will fill this out more.
2. Paulo Freire, *Pedagogy of the Oppressed* (New York: Seabury, 1970). pp. 19-24
3. H. Reudi Weber, *Experiments in Bible Study* (Geneva: WCC) ix.
4. P. Friere, op. cit.
5. The recovery of past biblical interpretation is similar to the interests of canon-canonical criticism. See the following works: J. Blenkinsopp, *Prophecy and Canon* (Notre Dame University Press, 1977); W. Brueggemann, *The Creative Word: Canon as a Model for Biblical Education* (Philadelphia: Fortress Press, 1982); B. Childs, *Introduction to the Old Testament as Scripture* (Philadelphia: Fortress Press, 1979); J. Sanders, *Canon and Community: A Guide to Canonical Criticism* (Philadelphia: Fortress Press, 1984); G. Sheppard, "Canonization: Hearing the Voice of the Same God Through

Historically Dissimilar Traditions," *Int* 37 (1982) 21-33. The background of the canon-canonical criticism debate is evident here. What Childs has done so that the present audience might appreciate the genius of John Calvin as a biblical interpreter now lays the foundation for a new appreciation of Sojourner Truth as a biblical interpreter.

6. Smith, *The Relational Self*, p. 21.

7. We could have used other forms such as visual art or dance, but those will have to wait for another volume.

Notes to Chapter 4

1. M. L. King, Jr., "Nobel Prize Acceptance Speech," in *A Testament of Hope. The Essential Writings of Martin* Luther King, Jr. ed. James M. Washington (San Francisco: Harper & Row, 1986).

2. This has been consistently challenged. Most recently by Cornel West, *Prophecy Deliverance. An Afro-American Revolutionary Christianity* (Philadelphia: Westminister, 1982), p. 16 and James Cone, *For My People. Black Theology and the Black Church* (Maryknoll: Orbis, 1984), pp. 175-178

3. Often the Hebrew *yam suf* is rendered Red Sea because church tradition connected the two. However, it does not represent a literal translation. Therefore, I prefer the more literal translation "reed sea."

4. This Afro-American spiritual has many more verses than are usually seen in print. William B. McClain identifies at least 18 verses detailing the trek from Egypt to the Promised Land in *Songs of Zion* (Nashville: Abingdon Press, 1981), pp. 112-113. See also his discussion of the spirituals in *Come Sunday: The Liturgy of Zion* (Nashville: Abingdon Press, 1990).

5. C.K. Dixon, *Negro Spirituals. From Bible to Folksong* (Philadelphia: Fortress, 1976), p. 22-23.

6. J.H. Cone, *The Spiritual and the Blues* (New York: Seabury, 1972) 13. pp. 13-19

7. P. Achtemeier, et al, *The Harper's Bible Dictionary* (San Francisco: 1985) "midrash," p. 635.

8. J.H. Cone, *Black Theology and Black Power* (New York: Seabury, 1969), pp. 79-81.

9. This is a matter of ethnic origin, Israel or Egypt, not a matter of class despite the class issues in the rest of the story.

10. Roberta Flack, Joel Dorn and Jesse Jackson, "Go Up, Moses," ASCAP 1971.

11. See the work of Franz Fanon, *Black Skins, White Masks* (New York: Grove, 1964).

12. The work done on the "divine warrior" in antiquity has failed to consider a black perspective. Few metaphors in recent biblical studies provide as much potential for a revolutionary black theology. See F.M.

Cross, *Canaanite Myth and Hebrew Epic. Essays in the History of the Religion of Israel* (Cambridge: Harvard, 1973), p. 91-111.

13. G. Coats, *Rebellion in the Wilderness. The Murmuring Motif in the Wilderness Traditions of the Old Testament* (Nashville: Abingdon, 1968), pp 13-17.

14. Ibid., p. 29.

Notes to Chapter 5

1. However, this theme is found in Mesopotamian (area now of Iraq) religion as early as the second millennium (2000 B.C.). Nonetheless, these seem more distant relatives.

2. J. L. Crenshaw, *Old Testament Wisdom: An Introduction* (Atlanta: John Knox, 1981), pp 100-148

3. C. Westermann, *The Structure of the Book of Job. A Form Critical Analysis* (Philadelphia: Fortress, 1981), pp. 4-6.

4. R.E. Murphy, *Wisdom Literature. Job, Proverbs, Ruth, Canticles Ecclesiastes, and Esther,* Vol. XIII: Forms of Old Testament Literature (Grand Rapids: Wm. B. Eerdmans, 1981), pp. 22-23.

5. C. Westerman, "The Role of Lament in Old Testament Theology."

6. C. Westerman, *The Structure of the Book of Job. A Form-Critical Analysis* (Philadelphia: Fortress, 1981), p. 34.

7. R. Gordis, *The Book of God and Man. A Study of Job* (Chicago: University of Chicago Press, 1965), p. 6.

8. H.W. Wolff, *Anthropology and the Old Testament* (Philadelphia: Fortress, 1974), pp 10-22.

9. M. Pope, *Job* (Anchor Bible), New York: Doubleday, 1982, p. 22.

10. R. Murphy, *Wisdom Literature. Job, Proverbs, Ruth, Canticles, Ecclesiastes, and Esther* (Grand Rapids: Wm. B. Eerdmans, 1981), p. 41.

11. M. Pope, *Job*, AB p. 347. There is a word missing in the Hebrew text which would provide the object from the verb, *ma'as*, reject. The RSV proposes that Job rejects himself. The result would be the translation, "I despise myself." In this literary context where speech and words play such a role, Pope argues that the missing object is "my [Job's] words." The resulting translation would be, "I recant and repent."

12. Urban renewal has dispersed the once strong black section of San Francisco, leaving the black community less of a political force in the city.

Glossary

anamnestic solidarity—bonding based on the process of recollection

application—the outline of the implications of the text for behavior, ethics

appropriate vulnerability—assessment of the risk of injury based on the possible rewards. Community affiliations and recollections inform this process

christus victor—the victorious Christ as the sovereign of the world

civil religion—religion organized primarily by civil and political affiliations. It has a bent toward the status quo. (See popular political theology.)

conscientization—a concept of Paulo Freire that involves raising the awareness of power relations in a culture. (See also critical reading, critical awareness)

critical awareness—a knowledge and experience of political structures that move against a given community

critical reading—examining the literary and ideological function of a text (See intrinsic reading.)

daimon—the literary device of the "other"

Exodus tradition—The stories about the events leading up to and following the Exodus.

extrinsic reading—examining of the text in light of other relevant texts and cultural artifacts such as music and visual arts

hermeneutics—rules of interpretation

hermeneutics of suspicion—a term popularized by Paul Ricoeur. The rules of interpretation in this case are formed by disbelief of the ostensible claims of the text

imitatio christi—the tradition of encouraging Christians to imitate the behavior of Jesus Christ

inclusio—a literary device that accents a theme by use of literary brackets

intrinsic reading—an examination of text on the basis of the text itself (See also critical reading.)

marginality—experience of limited power of social and political control

material life—the economic (i.e., money or land) and artifactual (i.e., housing, etc.) elements that structure human existence (See materialistic reading.)

materialistic reading—an examination of texts on the basis of the way economic and artifactual elements structure the themes of a particular text

partnership—state of being a person or community that takes part in action with others

patriotism—love of country and belief in the stated premise (i.e., stated beliefs) of the country

perspective—a worldview based on the interpretation of experience

pietism—a system that stresses the devotional aspect of religion (See also radicalism)

popular political theology—civil religion that finds broad grass root support

race pride—a catalyst for positive behavior due to identification with a particular race (See anamnestic solidarity)

radicalism—a system that stresses social change as a key aspect of religion (See also pietism)

recovery of black biblical tradition—the process of uncovering black texts and cultural artifacts that speak to biblical issues (See anamnestic solidarity)

structural poverty—poverty, due to economic structures, not merely unfortunate individual circumstances

theophany—appearance of God

unity—the awareness of the connection between material life and pietism and radicalism

Select Bibliography

Blenkinsopp, Joseph. *Prophecy and Canon*. Notre Dame: Notre Dame University Press, 1977.

Brueggemann, Walter. *The Creative Word. Canon as a Model for Biblical Education*. Philadelphia: Fortress, 1982.

Childs, Brevard. *Introduction to the Old Testament as Scripture*. Philadelphia: Fortress, 1979.

Clevenot, Michel. *Materialist Approaches to the Bible*. Maryknoll: Orbis, 1985.

Coats, George. *Rebellion in the Wilderness. The Murmuring Motif in the Wilderness Traditions of the Old Testament*. Nashville: Abingdon, 1968.

Cone, James H. *Black Theology and the Black Church*. Maryknoll: Orbis, 1984.

____. *For My People. Black Theology and the Black Church*. Maryknoll: Orbis, 1984.

____. *The Spiritual and the Blues*. New York: Seabury, 1972.

Crenshaw, James L. *Old Testament Wisdom: An Introduction*. Atlanta: John Knox, 1981.

Cross, Frank Moore. *Canaanite Myth and Hebrew Epic. Essays in the History of the Religion of Israel.* Cambridge: Harvard, 1973.

Dixon, C.K. *Negro Spirituals. From Bible to Folksong.* Philadelphia: Fortress, 1976.

DuBois, W.E.B. *Souls of Black Folk.* New York: Fawcett, 1961.

Eagleton, Terry. *Literary Theory: An Introduction.* Minneapolis: University of Minnesota, 1983.

Fanon, Franz. *Black Skins, White Masks.* New York: Grove, 1964.

Flack, Roberta, Joel Dorn, and Jesse Jackson, *Go Up, Moses*, ASCAP 1971.

Freire, Paulo. *Pedagogy of the Oppressed.* New York: Seabury, 1970.

Fuller, Charles. *A Soldier's Play.* New York: Hill and Wang, 1981.

Gordis, Robert. *The Book of God and Man. A Study of Job.* Chicago: University of Chicago Press, 1965.

Johnson, James Weldon. *God's Trombones.* New York: The Viking Press, 1964 [1927].

Knight, Douglas and Gene Tucker eds., *The Hebrew Bible and Its Modern Interpreters.* Philadelphia: Fortress/ Scholars Press, 1985.

Kraus, Hans Joachim. *Geschichte der historich-kritischen Erforschung des Alten Testaments.* Neukirch: Neukirchener Verlag, 1969.

Morrison, Toni. *The Bluest Eye.* New York: Washington Square Press, 1970.

____. *Tar Baby*. New York: New American Library, 1981.

Murphy, Roland E. *Wisdom Literature. Job, Proverbs, Ruth, Canticles Ecclesiastes, and Esther*. Vol. XIII, Forms of Old Testament Literature Grand Rapids: Wm. B. Eerdmans, 1981.

Pope, Marvin, *Job*. Anchor Bible 22. Doubleday: New York, 1982.

Reudi-Weber, Hans. *Experiments in Bible Study*. Geneva: WCC, 1970.

Sanders, James A. *Canon and Community: A Guide to Canonical Criticism*. Philadelphia: Fortress, 1984.

Sheppard, Gerald. "Canonization: Hearing the Voice of the Same God Through Historically Dissimilar Traditions," *Interpretation* 37 (1982) 21-33.

Smith, Archie, Jr. *The Relational Self. Ethics & Therapy from a Black Church Perspective*. Nashville: Abingdon, 1982.

Snowden, Frank M. Jr. *Blacks in Antiquity; Ethiopians in the Greco-Roman Experience*. Cambridge, Mass.: Belknap Press of Harvard University, 1970.

Walker, Alice. *The Color Purple*. New York: Washington Square Press, 1982.

____. *The Life of Grange Copeland*. New York: Harcourt, Brace Jovanovich, 1982.

Washington, James M. ed. *A Testament of Hope. The Essential Writings of Martin Luther King Jr.* San Francisco: Harper & Row, 1986.

West, Cornel. *Prophesy Deliverance. An Afro-American Revolutionary Christianity* (Philadelphia: Westminister, 1982)

Westermann, Claus. "The Role of Lament in Old Testament Theology," *Interpretation* Vol 38 January 1974.

Westermann, Claus. *The Structure of the Book of Job. A Form Critical Analysis.* Philadelphia: Fortress, 1981.

White, Hayden. *Metahistory. The Historical Imagination in Nineteenth-Century Europe.* Baltimore: Johns Hopkins, 1973.

Wolff, Hans Walter. *Anthropology and the Old Testament.* Philadelphia: Fortress, 1978.

For Further Reading

Cannon, Katie G. *Black Womanist Ethics.* Atlanta: Scholars Press, 1988.

Cone, James Hal. *For My People: Black Theology and the Black Church.* Maryknoll: Orbis, 1984.

_____. *My Soul Looks Back.* Maryknoll: Orbis, 1986.

Copher, Charles B. "3,000 Years of Biblical Interpretation with Reference to Black Peoples." *The Journal of the Interdenominational Theological Center,* vol. 13, no. 2 (Spring, 1986): 225-46.

Cummings, George. *Black Theology (U.S.A.) and Latin American Liberation Theology: Towards a Religio-Cultural, Socio-Economic and Political Theology of Liberation.* Maryknoll: Orbis, 1991.

Dunston, Alfred. *The Black Man in the Old Testament and Its World.* Philadelphia: Dorrance, 1974.

Felder, Cain ed. *Rocky the Road We Trod.* Philadelphia: Fortress, 1990.

Felder, Cain. *Troubling Biblical Waters. Race, Class, and Family* (Maryknoll: Orbis, 1989).

Franklin, Robert Michael. *Liberating Visions: Human Fulfillment and Social Justice in African-American Thought.* Philadelphia: Fortress, 1990.

Grant, Jacquelyn. *White Women's Christ, Black Women's Jesus.* Atlanta: Scholars, 1989.

Jones, Amos N. *Paul's Message of Freedom: What Does It Mean for the Black Church?* Valley Forge, PA: Judson, 1984.

Jones, William R. *Is God a White Racist? A Preamble to Black Theology.* Garden City, NY: Anchor Books, 1973.

Lincoln, C. Eric. *Race, Religion and the Continuing American Dilemma.* New York: Hill and Wang, 1984.

Long, Charles H. *Significations: Signs Symbols, and Images in the Interpretation of Religion.* Philadelphia: Fortress, 1986.

Paris, Peter. *The Social Teaching of the Black Churches.* Philadelphia: Fortress, 1985.

Raboteau, Albert J. *Slave Religion: The "Invisible Institution" in the Antebellum South.* New York: Oxford University Press, 1978.

Roberts, J. Deotis, *Black Political Theology.* Philadelphia: Westminster, 1974.

_____. *Black Theology in Dialogue.* Philadelphia: Westminster, 1987.

_____. *Black Theology Today: Liberation and Contextualization.* New York: Edwin Mellen, 1984.

_____. *Liberation and Reconciliation: A Black Theology.* Philadelphia: Westminster, 1971.

_____. *Roots of a Black Future. Family and Church.* Philadelphia: Westminster, 1980.

Smith, Archie Jr. *The Relational Self. Ethics & Therapy from a Black Church Perspective.* Nashville: Abingdon, 1982.

Spencer, Jon Michael. *Protest & Praise: Sacred Music of Black Religion.* Philadelphia: Fortress, 1990.

Thomas, Latta. *Biblical Faith and the Black American.* Valley Forge, PA.: Judson Press, 1986.

Washington, Joseph. *Black Religion: The Negro and Christianity in the United States.* Boston: Beacon Press, 1964.

Weems, Renita. *Just a Sister Away. A Womanist Vision of Women's Relationships in the Bible.* San Diego: LuraMedia, 1988.

West, Cornel. *Prophesy Deliverance. An Afro-American Revolutionary Christianity.* Philadelphia: Westminster, 1982.

Wilmore, Gayraud S. *Black Religion and Black Radicalism. An Interpretation of the Religious History of Afro-American People.* Second, Revised Enlarged Edition. Maryknoll: Orbis, 1983.

_____. ed. *African American Religious Studies*

Wimbush, Vincent. "Biblical-Historical Study as Liberation: Toward an Afro-Christian Hermeneutic." *The Journal of Religious Thought,* vol. 42, no. 2 (Fall-Winter, 1985-86).